10 Minute Guide to OS/2® 2.0

Herb Tyson

alpha
books

A Division of Prentice Hall Computer Publishing
11711 North College, Carmel, Indiana 46032 USA

© 1992 by Alpha Books

All rights reserved. No part of this book shall be reproduced, stored in a retrieval system, or transmitted by any means, electronic, mechanical, photocopying, recording, or otherwise, without written permission from the publisher. No patent liability is assumed with respect to the use of the information contained herein. Although every precaution has been taken in the preparation of this book, the publisher and author assume no responsibility for errors or omissions. Neither is any liability assumed for damages resulting from the use of the information contained herein. For information, address Alpha Books, 11711 N. College Ave., Carmel, IN 46032.

International Standard Book Number: 1-56761-000-5
Library of Congress Catalog Card Number: 92-72901

95 94 93 92   8 7 6 5 4 3 2 1

Interpretation of the printing code: The rightmost number of the first series of numbers is the year of the book's printing; the rightmost number of the second series of numbers is the number of the book's printing. For example, a printing code of 92-1 shows that the first printing of the book occurred in 1992.

Publisher: *Marie Butler-Knight*
Managing Editor: *Elizabeth Keaffaber*
Product Development Manager: *Lisa A. Bucki*
Acquisitions Editor: *Susan Klopfer*
Development Editor: *Seta Frantz*
Manuscript Editor: *Howard Peirce*
Cover Design: *Dan Armstrong*
Designer: *Michele Laseau*
Production Team: *Christine Cook, Dennis Clay Hager, John Kane, Carrie Keesling, Juli Pavey, Linda Quigley, Angie Trzepacz, Lisa Wilson*
Indexer: *Tina Trettin*

Screen reproductions in this book were created by means of the program Collage Plus from Inner Media, Inc., Hollis, NH.

Special thanks to Hilary J. Adams for ensuring the technical accuracy of this book.

Printed in the United States of America

Contents

Introduction, xi

1 Introducing the Workplace Shell, 1

Starting OS/2, 1
The Opening Screen, 3
The Desktop, 5
How to Shut Down, 6

2 Basic Mouse Navigation, 8

Using Mouse Buttons, 8
Pointing with the Mouse, 9
Clicking and Dragging, 9
Using the Window List, 11
Arranging Windows, 11
Using Object Pop-up Menus, 12
Desktop Pop-up Menu, 12
Other Object Pop-up Menus, 14

3 Controlling Objects with a Mouse, 15

Opening Objects, 15
Closing Objects, 16
Minimizing, Maximizing,
    and Restoring Object Windows, 17
Resizing Object Windows, 17
Moving Object Windows, 18
Using Scroll Bars, 19

4 Controlling Objects with the Keyboard, 21

Using Menus and Settings Screens, 21
Displaying the Window List, 23
Displaying Object Pop-up Menus, 23
Opening Objects, 24
Closing Objects, 24
Minimizing, Maximizing,
  and Restoring Object Windows, 24
Resizing Object Windows, 25
Moving Object Windows, 25

5 A Guided Tour of the Workplace Shell, 26

Displaying Different Views, 26
Icon View, 27
Tree View, 28
Details View, 29
The Default Desktop, 30
Start Here, 30
OS/2 System, 30
Information, 31
Master Help Index, 32
Templates Folder, 32
Printer, 32
Drive A, 32
Minimized Window Viewer, 32
Shredder, 33

6 Getting Help, 34

Using the F1 Key for Help, 34
Desktop Help, 35
Help for Other Objects, 35
Help for Menu Options and Push Buttons, 35
Using Master Help and the Information Folder, 36
Getting Help at the OS/2 Command Line, 39

Contents

7 Controlling OS/2 Behavior, 40

Changing the Keyboard, 40
Timing, 42
Mappings, 43
Special Needs, 43
General, 43
Changing the Mouse, 43
Timing, 44
Setup, 44
Mappings, 45
Switching Countries, 45
Controlling Sound, 45
Setting the System Clock, 46

8 Controlling OS/2's Appearance, 47

Using the Color Palette, 47
Using the Scheme Palette, 49
Editing an Existing Scheme, 49
Using the Font Palette, 51
Adding and Deleting Fonts, 52

9 Organizing the Desktop, 54

Migrating Applications, 54
Using Templates to Create Objects, 55
Using Folders, 56
Moving Objects Among Folders, 56
Copying Objects, 57
Copying versus Shadowing, 58
Using Selective Install, 58
Using Device Driver Install, 58

10 Understanding OS/2 File Systems, 60

What Is a File System?, 60
Understanding HPFS and FAT, 61
Finding Out If You Can Use HPFS, 62
What Are Extended Attributes?, 62
Where Are the EAs on a FAT Disk?, 63
Naming Files—Dos and Don'ts, 63

11 Displaying Directories with Drive Objects, 65

What Is a Drive Object?, 65
Displaying a Tree View, 66
Displaying an Icon View, 67
Displaying a Details View, 68
Formatting Diskettes with a Drive Object, 69

12 Copying Files and Folders with the Drive Object, 71

Copying from HPFS to FAT, 71
Copying from Folder to Folder, 73

13 Managing Files and Folders with the Drive Object, 75

Moving Objects, 75
Deleting Objects, 76
Undeleting Files, 77
Renaming Objects, 79
Creating Subdirectories, 80

14 Finding the OS/2 Command Prompt, 81

Command Line versus Object Orientation, 81
Opening an OS/2 Command Line Session, 82
Closing an OS/2 Command Line Session, 83
Opening Multiple OS/2 Command Line Sessions, 83

15 Using the OS/2 Command Line, 85

The OS/2 Command Line, 85
Running Programs, 85
Using Enhanced Filenames, 86
Editing the Command Line, 86
Using the Command Stack, 87
Editing Modes, 88
Getting Help, 88

16 Printing in OS/2, 91

OS/2 Print Interface, 91
Printing from Applications, 92
Printing Using Drag and Drop, 92
Understanding Printers and Spoolers, 93
Setting the Spooler Location, 94
Disabling the Spooler, 94
Enabling the Spooler, 95
Adding Printer Fonts, 95

17 Managing Print Jobs, 98

Print Jobs, 98
Using the Printer Object, 99
Reordering Printing, 99
Changing Printer Characteristics, 101

18 Editing Text, 104

OS/2 Editors, 104
Using the System Editor, 105
Editing Files, 105
Moving the Insertion Point, 106
Inserting Text, 107
Selecting Text, 107
Deleting Text, 108
Undo, 108
Saving Your Work, 109
Using the Clipboard, 109
Enhanced File Editor, 111

19 Managing Time with the Planning Applets, 112

Managing Time, 112
Integrating the Planning Applets, 112
Alarms, 115
Setting Alarms, 115
Monthly Planner, 116
Daily Planner, 117

Planner Archive, 118
Calendar, 118
Activities List, 118
Tune Editor, 119
To Do List, 119
To Do List Archive, 119
Database, 119

20 Touring the Productivity Applets, 120

Spreadsheet, 120
PM Chart, 120
Sticky Pad, 121
Picture Viewer, 121
PM Terminal, 122
System, 123
Pulse, 123
Icon Editor, 123
Seek and Scan Files (PM Seek), 124
Clipboard, 124

21 Running DOS in OS/2, 125

Emulating DOS 5, 125
Limitations of OS/2's DOS, 126
Opening a DOS Command
   Line Session, 126
Closing a DOS Command Line Session, 127
Working at the DOS
   Command Line, 127
Using AUTOEXEC.BAT, 128
Using the Clipboard in
   a DOS Session, 128
Using the Clipboard with a Mouse, 130

22 Running WIN–OS/2, 132

Running Windows, 132
Opening WIN-OS/2, 133

Closing WIN-OS/2, , 135
Setting the Display Method, 135
Running Alone versus Sharing WIN-OS/2, 136

23 Using and Managing WIN-OS/2, 138

Configuring a WIN-OS/2 Session, 138
Adding a Windows Application to a Folder, 139
Using the Clipboard in WIN-OS/2, 140
Printing in WIN-OS/2, 140
Using the Adobe Type Manager, 140
Adding ATM fonts, 142

A Up and Running with OS/2, 143

Using DISKCOPY to Make
  Backups of Program Disks, 143
Backing Up Your System Before Installing OS/2, 144
Different Types of Installation, 145
OS/2 only, 145
Dual Boot, 146
Boot Manager, 146
What's Best for You?, 146
Speed, 147
Running Multiple Operating Systems, 148
Uninstalling OS/2, 148
Removing OS/2 from an OS/2-Only System, 148
Removing OS/2 Files from a Dual Boot System, 149
Removing Boot Manager and HPFS Partitions, 150

B Summary of Common OS/2 Procedures, 151

Opening, Closing, Resizing,
  and Moving Windows (Lessons 3 and 4), 151
Navigating OS/2 (Lessons 3 and 4), 153
Copying, Shadowing, and Deleting
  an Object (Lessons 9, 12, and 13), 155
Creating and Renaming Objects (Lessons 13 and 16), 157

C Command Reference, 160

Index, 181

Introduction

You're probably reading this book because you've either just taken the OS/2 plunge or are just about to. You're in for an exciting trip. In the past ten or eleven years, personal computing hardware went through some amazing technological leaps. Yet, during the same period, the fundamental operating system (DOS) changed very little. Computers have gotten faster and bigger, but have not really gotten much better—until now. With OS/2 2.0, there's finally an operating system built to take advantage of your advanced hardware.

What Is OS/2 2.0?

OS/2 2.0 is an advanced set of programs for 80386 and 80486 computers that provides access to a computer's resources. OS/2 offers the Workplace Shell, which lets you control your computer by clicking on small pictures that represent computer resources and operations. You control your computer using these small pictures rather than commands and files.

With OS/2 2.0, you can:

- Run OS/2, DOS, and Windows programs.

- Run more than one program at a time.

- Take full advantage of your 80386 or 80486 computer.

Why the *10 Minute Guide to OS/2 2.0?*

You want to get up and running with OS/2 2.0 as quickly as possible. To do this, a few things are certain:

- You need to be able to find your way around OS/2 quickly and easily.

- You need to identify and learn the tasks necessary for you to accomplish your particular goals.

- You need a clear-cut, plain-English guide to the essential features of OS/2 2.0.

  You need the *10 Minute Guide to OS/2 2.0*.

  The *10 Minute Guide to OS/2 2.0* will quickly get you started in OS/2 2.0. It points out basic methods and resources, while at the same time alerting you to possible traps and snags. You can complete each lesson in approximately 10 minutes. If you go through the whole book, you'll be up to speed in about half a day.

Conventions Used in This Book

This book uses these conventions to help you move through the lessons easily:

`On-screen text`	On-screen text will appear in a special computer font.

What you type	Information you type will appear in a bold, color, computer font.
Items you select	Commands, options, and icons you select or keys you press will appear in color.
Selection keys	Boldface letters within a menu or window option indicate selection keys for keyboard shortcuts. These correspond to the underlined letters on-screen.

In addition to these conventions, the *10 Minute Guide to OS/2 2.0* uses three special symbols to identity helpful information:

Plain English   New or unfamiliar terms are defined in plain English.

Timesaver Tips   Methods that cut corners and confusion.

Panic Button   This symbol identifies areas that often cause confusion or panic, and offers practical solutions.

Trademarks

All known trademarks or services marks mentioned in this book are listed below. The publisher cannot attest to the accuracy of this information. Use of a term in this book should not be regarded as affecting the validity of any trademark or service mark.

> AmiPro and Lotus are registered trademarks of Lotus Development Corporation.
>
> DeScribe is a registered trademark of DeScribe, Inc.
>
> Excel, WinWord and Windows are registered trademarks of Microsoft Corporation.
>
> FAXability is a trademark of Intel Corporation.
>
> LaserJet is a registered trademark of Hewlett-Packard Company.
>
> IBM and OS/2 are registered trademarks of International Business Machines Corporation.
>
> MailReader/2 is a trademark of Knight Writer Software Company.
>
> Signature is a registered trademark of Xyquest, Inc.
>
> TurboTax is a registered trademark of Chipsoft CA, Corp.
>
> WinFax is a registered trademark of Delrina, Inc.

Lesson 1
Introducing the Workplace Shell

In this lesson, you'll learn how to start and quit OS/2. You will also learn the parts of the Workplace Shell's Desktop screen.

Starting OS/2

OS/2 is an *operating system*. To start it, just turn on your computer. If you installed dual boot, use the following steps to start OS/2 from DOS:

1. Close any open programs.

2. Type C:\OS2\BOOT /OS2.

   If you installed the boot manager:

1. When the boot selection menu appears, use the cursor keys to select OS/2 2.0.

2. Press Enter.

1

Lesson 1

What's Dual Boot? *Dual boot* is an OS/2 installation option that lets you keep OS/2 and DOS on the same hard disk partition. To switch from DOS to OS/2, use the procedure shown above. To switch from OS/2 to DOS, double-click the Boot DOS object in the Command Prompts folder.

I'd Like to See the Manager The Boot Manager is an OS/2 installation option that lets you keep multiple operating systems (for example, DOS, OS/2 2.0, OS/2 1) on the same computer system. When Boot Manager is installed, you select an operating system each time your computer is turned on or rebooted.

When booting, the OS/2 logo appears (it looks like the Olympic rings). After about two minutes, the initial Desktop screen appears (see Figure 1.1).

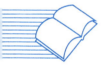
What's an Operating System? An *operating system* is a set of detailed computer programs that control your computer. The operating system controls how your computer system's components work together: disks, keyboard, mouse, memory, monitor, and so on.

Long Boots OS/2 is an advanced operating system that controls a lot more of your computer system than you might be used to. In order to work, OS/2 has to preload a number of instructions into your computer's memory. This process is called *booting*. OS/2 is a disk manager, a memory manager, a keyboard manager, a mouse manager, a CD (compact disc) manager, a communications

Introducing the Workplace Shell

manager, a fax manager, a program manager—you get the idea. OS/2 loads control programs for each of these—and more—each time you boot OS/2. The more powerful the operating system, the longer the boot takes.

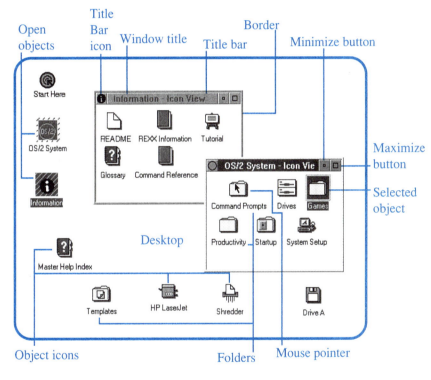

Figure 1.1 The opening OS/2 Desktop screen.

The Opening Screen

As shown in Figure 1.1, the Desktop consists of a number of components. You will use these components throughout OS/2 and OS/2 applications. The components of the opening screen include:

Lesson 1

Desktop The Desktop is the area that contains all the other objects in the Workplace Shell.

Object Icons Object icons represent *folders, programs, data files,* and *devices.* Everything in OS/2 is an object—including the Desktop (a folder object).

Icons, Folders, and Devices An *icon* is a small computer picture that indicates the purpose of an object. (A printer is represented by a small picture of a printer. A folder looks like a small manila folder. And the System Editor is represented by a picture of a pencil.) A *folder* is any object that contains other objects. You use folders to group related programs and files together. Folders are similar to the subdirectories used in DOS. *Devices* include things like printers, scanners, plotters, and modems.

Mouse Pointer You use the mouse pointer to select and manipulate objects and commands.

Open Object Diagonal lines across an object icon indicate that a copy of that object is being used (is open).

Selected Object Shading indicates that an object is selected; you perform actions on objects by selecting objects and then choosing an action.

Figure 1.1 also shows two open windows. A *window* is a screen area used to display an open object (an open object is also called a *task*). The main components of an OS/2 window are:

Title Bar Icon This is "command central" for every OS/2 window—used to control the program, window, and settings.

Window Title The name of the object that's displayed in the window.

Title Bar Often gives more information about the open window, such as a document name or a specific subtask.

Borders Indicate the four sides of a window.

Minimize Button Reduces a window to an object icon (minimizing puts an object window out of the way, but it doesn't close it—see Lesson 3).

Maximize Button Expands a window to its maximum size. Some windows can fill the entire screen. Other windows are programmed so that they fill up only a portion of the screen.

What's a Window? A *window* on-screen acts like a window in a house. You can look through someone's living room window to see if anyone's home. In the same way, you can view an object's window to see what it contains.

The Desktop

When OS/2 is installed, a number of objects are available for immediate use. The default Desktop arrangement is shown in Figure 1.1. The Desktop is the first layer of objects in OS/2. Instead of executing programs and working with files on disk, you now use objects on or in your Desktop.

Your actual physical desk (the one you sit at) may contain some manila folders, a pad and pencil, some reference books, a pair of scissors, and so on. In the same way,

Lesson 1

your on-screen Desktop might contain folders, a printer, a source of help, and a Shredder. You perform all work on the Desktop. As you open windows to run programs, those windows may cover up all or part of the Desktop. The Desktop is nevertheless still there. The more cluttered your Desktop becomes, the more appropriate the new way of thinking seems!

How to Shut Down

To start OS/2, you just turn on your computer. To stop it, however, don't just turn off your computer. Instead, to maintain the integrity of your files, you must perform a *system shut down*. To shut down your system:

1. Save and close any open data or document files (follow the instructions for each application for saving data and document files).

2. Close any open objects or applications that you don't want automatically restarted the next time you boot OS/2 (you will learn to close OS/2 objects in Lesson 3).

3. Move the mouse pointer so that it points at any blank area on the Desktop, and then click (quickly press and release) mouse button 2 (usually the right button).

4. Move the mouse pointer over the Shut down option and click mouse button 1 (usually the left button).

5. Point the mouse at OK, and click mouse button 1 to confirm (in other words, you use the mouse to "push" the OK button).

6. When the message Shut down is complete appears, turn off your computer.

Introducing the Workplace Shell

File Allocation Errors? If you fail to properly shut down your system, OS/2 may advise you of file errors the next time you turn on your system. Usually, OS/2 corrects all problems automatically. If your system fails to start properly, contact IBM or your system support person. Usually, you will be told how to correct the problem by running CHKDSK /F on your hard disk.

Keep It That Way When performing a system shut down, you can deliberately leave some objects (folders and applications) open. OS/2 automatically reopens those objects the next time you start OS/2. Window positions and sizes are restored also. This keeps you from having to manually reestablish your Desktop each time you start OS/2.

In this lesson, you learned how to start and quit OS/2. You also learned the parts of the main OS/2 screen. In the next lesson, you will learn how to use your mouse.

Lesson 2
Basic Mouse Navigation

In this lesson, you will learn the basics of using the mouse in OS/2, and how to access and control the window list and the object pop-up menus.

Using Mouse Buttons

The mouse has a primary button (button 1) and a secondary button (button 2). By default, the left button is primary and the right button is secondary. Use button 1 to perform actions and to select and open objects. Use button 2 to manipulate objects.

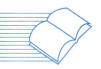

What's an Object? An *object* is any folder, program, data file, or device (such as a printer or shredder). You run OS/2 by doing things with objects. It might seem a little strange if you came to OS/2 from DOS, thinking of everything in terms of files. Then again, deleting or printing a file once seemed strange, too. A folder object is like a subdirectory. When you open a folder, you see what's in it.

Basic Mouse Navigation

Pointing with the Mouse

You point at objects and other parts of the screen by moving the mouse pointer onto them. When the mouse pointer is on an object, a list, a button, or other screen part that can be selected, it looks like an arrow (see Figure 2.1). When the mouse pointer is on a window border, it's a double-headed arrow (see Figure 2.2). When editing text, the mouse pointer is an I-beam (see Figure 2.3).

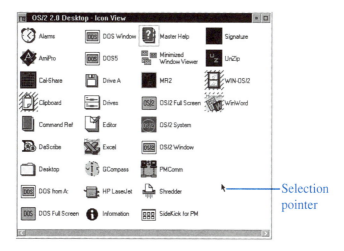

Selection pointer

Figure 2.1 The mouse pointer when selecting objects.

Clicking and Dragging

To *click* on something means that you quickly press and release a mouse button while the mouse pointer is positioned over an object, screen part, icon, or word. In this book, click mouse button 1 unless a different button is

Lesson 2

specified. In a list or a folder, a single click selects or highlights the item at the mouse pointer. When you point at a button, a click "pushes" the button, causing it to carry out a command.

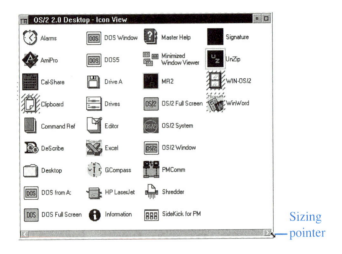

Figure 2.2 The mouse pointer when resizing a window.

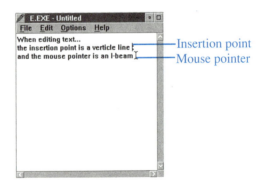

Figure 2.3 The mouse pointer in edit mode.

10

To *double-click,* you move the mouse pointer onto an object or a menu option, and press and release mouse button 1 twice in rapid succession. A double-click selects the option or item under the mouse pointer and causes an action to occur (for example, open or close an object). If you click on an object icon with button 1, you select it. If you double-click it, you select *and* open it. Always double-click using mouse button 1.

To *drag* the mouse, you move the pointer onto the object you want to drag, press and hold a mouse button (usually button 2), and then move the mouse without releasing the button. When the object icon or screen part is in its desired location, you release the mouse button to *drop* the object or fix the new location. You can drag object icons, window borders, and windows.

Using the Window List

In OS/2, a number of windows can be open at any given moment. The Window list lets you switch among and control open windows. To see the Window list:

- Click mouse buttons 1 and 2 at the same time on any blank area on the Desktop.

    To switch to any open window in the list:

- Double-click on the title of the window you want to switch to.

Arranging Windows

You can use the Window list to arrange selected tasks for access and viewing on the same screen. To arrange tasks:

Lesson 2

1. Display the Window list by clicking mouse buttons 1 and 2 on the Desktop.

2. Hold down the Ctrl key and click mouse button 1 on the title of each listed window you want to arrange. Release the Ctrl key when finished selecting.

3. Click mouse button 2 on the title of any selected window.

4. Click on the Tile or Cascade option.

Tiled Windows *Tiling* arranges windows so that each fits into its own rectangle on-screen. When you tile windows, you can see what's happening in different windows at the same time.

Cascading Windows *Cascading* arranges windows so that they overlap on-screen. Because they overlap, each viewing area can be larger than when windows are tiled, but you can view only the contents of the top window.

Using Object Pop-up Menus

Every object in OS/2 has its own pop-up menu for opening, closing, and controlling settings. When you display an object's pop-up menu, OS/2 presents a list of options.

Desktop Pop-up Menu

The Desktop pop-up menu lets you control the display of the Desktop and provides access to the Shut **d**own command. To see the Desktop's pop-up menu:

Basic Mouse Navigation

1. Move the mouse pointer to a blank area on the Desktop.

2. Click mouse button 2 to display the Desktop pop-up menu (see Figure 2.4).

Figure 2.4 The Desktop pop-up menu options.

The Desktop pop-up menu's options are:

Open   Offers different Desktop views and settings.

Refresh   Updates the display of the Desktop.

Help   Provides help with using the Desktop.

Create **s**hadow   Creates a shadow of the Desktop.

The Shadow Knows!   A *shadow* is a linked copy of an object. When you change a shadow, OS/2 changes the original object and any other shadows, too.

Lockup now   Blocks access to an active OS/2 system using password protection.

Shut **d**own   Shuts down before turning off or rebooting your computer.

Find   Lets you locate any object on the Desktop.

13

Lesson 2

Select   Lets you select or deselect all objects on the Desktop.

Sort   Lets you sort and set the sorting criteria for objects displayed.

Arrange   Rearranges objects on the Desktop.

Other Object Pop-up Menus

To display an open object's pop-up menu:

- Click either mouse button on the object's Title Bar icon.

To display an unopened object's pop-up menu:

- Click button 2 on the object.

Object pop-up menus are *context-sensitive*. That is, the menu displayed depends on the object and whether or not the object is open. When you select multiple objects, the pop-up menu displays options common to the selected objects.

Context-Sensitive?   A *context-sensitive* menu's contents change depending on what you're doing. If a single object is selected, you see its menu. If two objects are selected and one of them can't be deleted, then a common menu that omits the Delete option is presented. A context-sensitive menu presents only the options that apply to a particular situation.

In this lesson, you learned how to use the mouse. You also learned to display and use the window list and object pop-up menus. In the next lesson, you will learn how to use the mouse to control windows.

Lesson 3
Controlling Objects with a Mouse

In this lesson, you will learn how to open, close, minimize, maximize, restore, resize, and move object windows, and how to use scroll bars.

Opening Objects

The Workplace Shell (WPS) is a collection of objects arranged on the Desktop. Opening an object means different things for different objects: folder objects are displayed, program objects are started, data objects are loaded, and device objects perform actions. To open an object:

1. Point the mouse at the icon that represents the object.

2. Double-click mouse button 1.

The Workplace Shell   That's the name OS/2 2.0 gives to a program called PMSHELL.EXE. Similar to Windows' Program Manager and OS/2 1.3's Desktop Manager, the Workplace Shell organizes your programs and files. Windows' Program Manager lets you organize programs and files into program groups. The Workplace Shell lets you

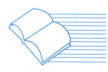

15

Lesson 3

organize your programs and files into folders. The main folder in the Workplace Shell is the Desktop.

Closing Objects

There is a uniform method for closing all OS/2 programs. However, the procedures for safely closing DOS and Windows programs vary by program. See each program's documentation for specific information on closing.

To close an OS/2 object:

- If the object has a menu, use its Close or Exit command (often File Exit or File Close).

or

- Double-click on the Title Bar icon.

You can also close objects using the object's pop-up menu or the Window list.

To Each Its Own When a program (especially a DOS or Windows program) has its own Close command, use it instead of OS/2's menus and controls. Failure to terminate a program according to its own rules can result in data loss or corruption. Use OS/2's Close controls on such programs only when the program fails to respond to its own Close command (for example, when the program becomes *hung*—that is, it no longer responds to its commands).

Minimizing, Maximizing, and Restoring Object Windows

When you minimize a window, OS/2 displays it as an icon, either on the Desktop or in the minimized window viewer. To minimize an object, click on the Minimize button.

When you maximize a window, OS/2 displays it in the maximum screen area defined for that object. To maximize an object, click on the Maximize button.

Windows can exist in three states: maximized, minimized, and restored. The normal state is restored. To restore a window, double-click on the title bar or on its icon.

Resizing Object Windows

To resize a window:

1. Move the mouse pointer so that it is on the border you want to adjust. When it is correctly positioned on the border, the mouse cursor becomes a double-headed arrow.

2. Move the mouse pointer over the window border so that it becomes a double-headed arrow.

3. Press and hold either mouse button and drag (move the mouse while holding down a button) the window border to a new position.

4. Release the mouse button when the window border is where you want it to be.

5. Repeat for all dimensions you want to adjust.

Lesson 3

Two for One You can change two dimensions simultaneously by dragging any of the four corners of an object window. When you position the mouse pointer on a corner, it displays as a diagonal double-headed arrow.

Moving Object Windows

You can move OS/2 objects anywhere you like as long as they are less than full screens. To move an object that is not maximized:

1. Position the mouse anywhere in the title bar.

2. Drag the whole window to the new location, using either mouse button.

    To move a minimized icon on the Desktop:

1. Point the mouse at the icon.

2. Drag the icon to the new location using either mouse button.

    To move a closed object icon in a folder or on the Desktop:

1. Point the mouse at the icon.

2. Drag the icon to the new location using mouse button 2.

Where Did It Go? When displaying multiple folders, it's easy to accidentally misplace icons. If you drag an icon from the Desktop to a folder or between folders, the structure of your Desktop will change. Sometimes this is exactly what you want to do—sometimes not. So be careful. If you lose an icon, use the Desktop pop-up menu's Find command to find it. For more on using the Find command, see Lesson 2, "Basic Mouse Navigation."

Using Scroll Bars

When an object's contents will not fit in the displayed window, OS/2 automatically displays scroll bars. Scroll bars let you change the view to see different parts of the object.

Figure 3.1 shows scroll bars in the Editor window. The position of the scroll box tells you the position of the current view relative to the whole object. Use the horizontal scroll bar to see more to the left and right. Use the vertical scroll bar to see more to the top and bottom. To use the scroll bars:

- Click a scroll arrow to gradually scroll the view of the object.

- Click in the scroll bar itself to scroll one screenful at a time.

- Drag the scroll box to a location relative to the section you want to view. For example, to view an area two-thirds of the way through a file, drag the scroll box two-thirds of the way down the vertical scroll bar.

Lesson 3

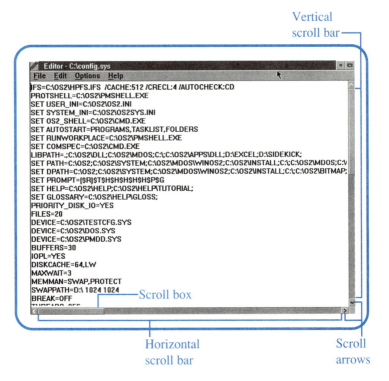

Figure 3.1 Using scroll bars to control the view.

In this lesson, you learned how to control Workplace Shell windows using a mouse. In the next lesson, you'll learn to do some of the same operations using the keyboard.

Lesson 4
Controlling Objects with the Keyboard

> In this lesson, you will learn keyboard techniques for controlling the Desktop and objects.

The Workplace Shell (WPS) is designed to be used with a mouse. You can also accomplish most actions with the keyboard. Learning the basic keystrokes can help you work faster in OS/2 by letting you keep your hands on the keyboard when you're performing a keyboard-intensive task.

Using Menus and Settings Screens

Many OS/2 actions, settings, and options are controlled using pop-up menus and screens. Most menus and screens can be controlled using keyboard shortcuts. Use the following keys to move around OS/2 screens. See Figure 4.1 for an example.

Tab Selects each distinct option from top to bottom, left to right (for example, in Figure 4.1, press Tab to select Copies, Orientation, Fast system fonts, Resolution, Paper feed, Form, and so on, in that order).

Lesson 4

Shift-Tab   Selects each distinct option from bottom to top, right to left. In other words, press Shift-Tab to move back through the cycle that you move through when you press Tab.

Key Combinations   Many keyboard shortcuts require you to press more than one key at the same time. In this book, such key combinations are shown as two or more keys joined by a hyphen. For example, when you see the key combination Shift-Tab, press and hold the Shift key, press Tab, and release both keys. Sometimes you need to press two or more keys in sequence. If, for example, you see the key sequence Alt, F, press and release the Alt key and then press F.

Arrow Keys   Use the arrow (cursor) keys to select among options in any section of a menu, list, or set of buttons.

Space Bar   Press the space bar to select and deselect objects and options.

Enter   Press the Enter key to execute a selected push-button command (OK, **E**ffects, **C**ancel, or **H**elp, in Figure 4.1).

Selection Letters   If letters are underlined on-screen, you can select the corresponding option by pressing the underlined letter on the keyboard (for example, press P to select Portrait, or L to select Landscape). Selection letters are indicated in **bold** throughout this book. If the cursor is in a text area, press and hold the Alt key and press the selection letter to select keyboard shortcuts. In a list box, you can select an item by pressing its initial letter.

22

Controlling Objects with the Keyboard

Alt-↓   Press Alt-↓ to expand a list box so that multiple items can be viewed at the same time.

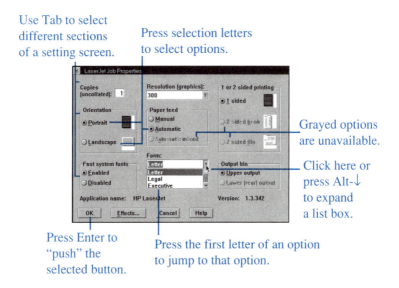

Figure 4.1   Using keys to control the Printer Properties Settings screen.

Displaying the Window List

To display the Window list, press Ctrl-Esc.

Displaying Object Pop-up Menus

To display the Desktop pop-up menu:

- Press Alt-Shift-Tab to make the Desktop active.

- Press Ctrl-\ to deselect all objects.

23

Lesson 4

- Press Shift-F10 to activate the Desktop pop-up menu.

  To display other object pop-up menus:

1. Select the object.

2. Press Shift-F10 to activate the Desktop pop-up menu.

Opening Objects

To open an object:

1. Press Alt-Esc to select the folder that contains the object you want.

2. Use the cursor keys to move to the object.

3. Press the space bar to select the object.

4. Press Enter to open the selected object.

Closing Objects

To close an object or window:

- Press Alt-F4.

Minimizing, Maximizing, and Restoring Object Windows

To minimize a window:

- Press Alt-F9.

To maximize a window:

- Press Alt-F10.

To restore a window:

- Press Alt-F5.

Resizing Object Windows

To resize a window:

1. Press Alt-F8.

2. Use the cursor keys to resize the window.

3. Press Esc when finished.

Moving Object Windows

To move a window:

1. Press Alt-F7.

2. Use the cursor keys to move the window where you want it.

3. Press Esc when you're done.

In this lesson, you learned how to navigate and manipulate OS/2 with the keyboard. In the next lesson, you can put those skills to work discovering all of the resources contained in the Workplace Shell.

Lesson 5

A Guided Tour of the Workplace Shell

In this lesson, you will learn how the Workplace Shell is organized, how to look at it in different ways, and which folders to open for specific tools.

The Workplace Shell (WPS) is IBM's name for OS/2's interface. OS/2 lets you use the WPS in a variety of ways. For starters, OS/2 lets you look at open objects in any of several ways, called *views*.

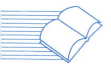

Face to Face An *interface* is the way you control a computer program. Some programs have a command interface, which requires that you type instructions. DOS's command line is a command interface. OS/2 has a graphical user interface—which means that you use pictures (graphics) of objects (programs, files, folders, and devices) to control OS/2.

Displaying Different Views

You can display most folders in three ways:

- Icon view

- Tree view
- Details view

Icon View

The first time you boot OS/2, you see a screen similar to the one shown in Figure 5.1. This view is an Icon view of your Desktop folder, with the Information and System folders open. The default Icon view is easy to read and use because it displays objects graphically, using icons.

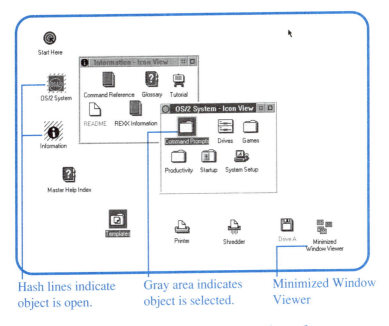

Figure 5.1 OS/2's opening screen, just after installation.

Lesson 5

Tree View

To see the Desktop in Tree view:

1. Click mouse button 2 on any blank area on the Desktop to display the Desktop pop-up menu.

2. Click on the arrow to the right of the word **Open**.

3. Select Tree view.

You now have the view shown in Figure 5.2, and you can scroll through the Desktop directory. It's a little clearer now that this mysterious thing called the Desktop is really nothing more than a directory of the available resources (see Lesson 11).

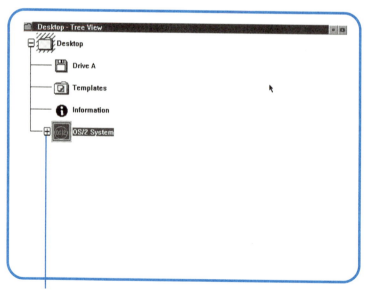

A plus sign indicates that this folder contains subfolders.

Figure 5.2 Tree view of the Desktop folder.

Details View

Another view of the Desktop is the Details view. To display the Details view:

1. Click mouse button 2 on any blank area on the Desktop to display the Desktop pop-up menu.

2. Click on the arrow to the right of the word **O**pen.

3. Select Details view.

This produces the view in Figure 5.3. Now you see detailed information about the objects on your Desktop, such as the real name and size. The Details view is very useful when performing directory management tasks (see Lesson 11).

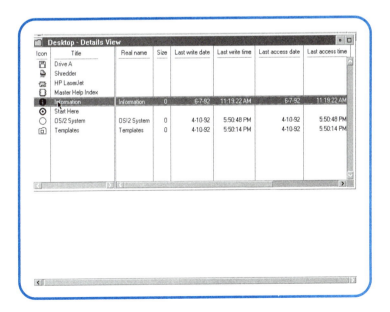

Figure 5.3   Details view of the Desktop folder.

Lesson 5

The Default Desktop

The first time you use OS/2, the basic resources available are those shown in Figure 5.1. These include three special folders (OS/2 System, Information, and Templates), as well as a very basic introduction (Start Here), a procedures lookup (Master Help Index), a printer, a Shredder (for deleting things), and a way to see what's on drive A. Beneath the surface, there's much more—the OS/2 System folder contains six subfolders. The Information folder contains five reference tools. If all this were spread out before you, it would be a very cluttered Desktop indeed! Each Desktop object is summarized below.

Start Here

The Start Here icon contains a short OS/2 introductory lesson. All users should take it, regardless of prior computer experience. OS/2 2.0 is fundamentally different from every other operating environment. It pays to learn the basics as early as possible.

OS/2 System

The OS/2 System folder (which doesn't look like a folder at all) contains all of the OS/2 system-related resources and tools. The OS/2 System folder contains at least six subfolders:

> **Drives** The Drives object is the primary disk and directory management tool.
>
> **Startup** A user-defined folder containing objects you want to initiate at start-up.

System Setup   System configuration and setup tools.

Command Prompts   OS/2 command prompts, DOS command prompts, WIN-OS/2 Full Screen, and dual boot to real DOS (if installed).

Games   Solitaire, chess, and four other games to help you learn OS/2 skills.

Productivity   Two dozen applications and utilities that come with OS/2.

If you let OS/2 install your existing OS/2, DOS, or Windows programs, then the system folder will contain additional program folders.

Information

Early on, many OS/2 users discover that the array of printed documents that comes with OS/2 is limited. There is no command reference, and no detailed manual on how to use OS/2. Instead, OS/2's documentation is on-line in the Master Help Index and the Information folder. The Information folder includes the following objects:

Glossary   Use it to look up OS/2-related terms.

Tutorial   Use the tutorial to acquire basic OS/2 skills.

Command Reference   The Command Reference tells you how to use (nearly) all of OS/2's commands.

REXX Information   Use this guide to learn about the REXX procedures language.

Lesson 5

Master Help Index

The Master Help Index is a heavily cross-referenced tool for learning OS/2 procedures. See Lesson 6 to learn how to use the Master Help Index.

Templates Folder

The Templates folder contains a number of object models. You use object models to create new objects. See Lesson 9 to learn how to use templates.

Printer

Use the printer object to print documents. You also can use it to configure the printer, the print queue, the destination of print jobs (file, LPT, COM, and so on), and the communications ports. You will learn more about printers in Lessons 16 and 17.

Drive A

You use the Drive A object to access drive A for installing software and copying data from disks.

Minimized Window Viewer

You can use the Minimized Window Viewer (MWV) to view all active minimized program objects, depending on your system setup.

Shredder

Use the Shredder to delete objects. See Lesson 13 for more on how to use the Shredder.

In this lesson, you learned how to find all of OS/2's built-in resources. Next, you'll learn how to use OS/2's help facilities.

Lesson 6
Getting Help

In this lesson, you'll learn the many ways to yell "Help!" in OS/2.

OS/2 contains a number of built-in help facilities. Specific help is usually just a keystroke away.

Using the F1 Key for Help

Almost everywhere, you can get context-sensitive help by pressing the F1 key. This is true not only when performing OS/2-related tasks, but when using most PM and Windows programs as well.

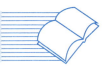

Who's Calling the Shots? *Presentation Manager* (*PM*) is the set of computer programs that gives OS/2 its graphical look—buttons, scroll bars, windows, and so on. OS/2 programs that don't have a graphical look are character based. Programs that have the graphical look are called *PM*. PM is to OS/2 what the Windows "look and feel" is to DOS.

Perle Systems Limited

Cordially invites you to attend a Wine and Cheese Presentation

"Sixth Annual Service Awards"

Thursday, April 28, 1994,

3:00 P.M.

in CAP's New Offices,

Suite 230, 2nd Floor,

60 Renfrew Drive

PLEASE JOIN US

erle

Desktop Help

To summon Desktop help:

1. Press Alt-Shift-Tab to make the Desktop active.

2. Press Ctrl-\ to deselect any objects that have been selected.

3. Press F1.

One at a Time The *active window* is the one that responds to current keyboard input. At any one time, only one window or object can be active.

Help for Other Objects

To get help for any object on the Desktop:

1. Click on the object.

2. Press F1.

Help for Menu Options and Push Buttons

You also can use the F1 key to get help on selected options from some menus. To get help for push buttons and menu options:

1. Point the mouse at the button or option.

2. Press and hold either mouse button.

3. Without releasing the mouse button, press the F1 key.

35

Lesson 6

Using Master Help and the Information Folder

The Master Help Index is OS/2's most thorough help resource. It provides an alphabetic listing of tasks and topics. To open the Master Help Index:

- Double-click on the Master Help Index object on the Desktop. You will see the window shown in Figure 6.1.

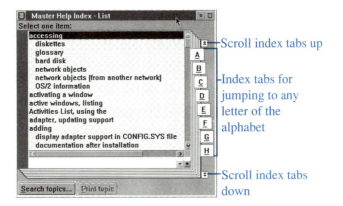

Figure 6.1 The Master Help Index main index window.

There are several ways to use the Master Help Index. To jump to a specific letter of the alphabet:

- Press the first letter of the topic you want.

  or

- Use the index tab scroll bar to display the letter you want.

Getting Help

To search for a topic by name:

1. Click on the Search topics button.

2. Type the name of the topic in the Search string: box.

3. Press Enter.

For example, to search for help about printing, type the word `printing` in the Search string: box. Now you see a list of topics that mention the word *printing*, as shown in Figure 6.2. To display help for any topic listed:

- Double-click on the topic.

Figure 6.2 The results of a search in the index.

Wild-Card Searches The search function works only on whole words. A search for `print` does not match `printing`. To widen the search, type the wild-card character * (asterisk) at the end of your search string. The search text `print*` matches `print`, `printer`, `printing`, and so on. The asterisk is the only wild card allowed in Help searches.

Lesson 6

In a topic window (a window in which a topic is explained or expanded), some words shown are highlighted in a special color or typeface. (In Figure 6.3, for example, OS/2* and Windows** are highlighted in the topic window.) The highlighted words are *hot links* to other areas of the help system.

What's a Hot Link? A *hot link* is a highlighted keyword in a topic window. If you double-click on a hot link, another topic window appears which provides detailed information and/or definitions of highlighted words. This way of presenting information sometimes is also called *hypertext*.

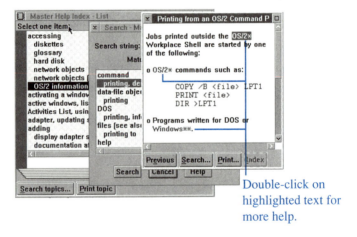

Double-click on highlighted text for more help.

Figure 6.3 The Printing from an OS/2 Command Prompt topic window.

To display help for a highlighted topic:

- Double-click mouse button 1 on the highlighted topic.

To back up to a previous help level or topic:

- Press Esc or click on the Previous button located beneath the help text.

Getting Help at the OS/2 Command Line

Sometimes when OS/2 encounters an error, it notifies you with a SYS error message box. Often, the SYS error pop-up message box contains a Help button. You can click on the Help button for further information.

If the SYS error pop-up does not contain a Help button, you can display additional information about the error by typing **HELP** followed by the SYS error number at the command line. For more on using OS/2 command lines, see Lesson 15.

In this lesson, you learned how to use OS/2's main help facilities. In the next lesson, you'll start learning how to control OS/2 to optimize your computerized work environment.

Lesson 7
Controlling OS/2 Behavior

In this lesson, you will learn how to control how OS/2 uses the keyboard, mouse, sound, and clock. You'll also learn how to change country settings and where OS/2 puts your spooler file.

Changing the Keyboard

To change the way the keyboard behaves, open the keyboard object. To open the keyboard object:

1. Double-click on the System Setup folder icon (see Figure 7.1), which is on the Desktop.

2. Double-click on the Keyboard object to open it (see Figure 7.2).

This window contains a notebook with four pages of settings, from which you can make a number of keyboard changes.

Notebooks Every OS/2 object has its own settings *notebook*. Each notebook is divided into one

Controlling OS/2 Behavior

or more *tabs*. Tabs are shown on the right side of the notebook (for example, **T**iming, **M**appings, **S**pecial Needs, and **G**eneral are tabs used in Figure 7.2). You move to different tabs by clicking on the tab you want to see. Some tabs are further divided into notebook pages. You move to different pages by clicking on the left and right page control arrows at the bottom of the notebook. When a tab contains multiple pages, text appears under the page control arrows to indicate the current and total pages (for example, Page 1 of 3).

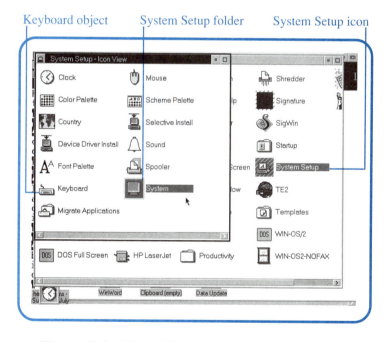

Figure 7.1 The initial System Setup folder.

41

Lesson 7

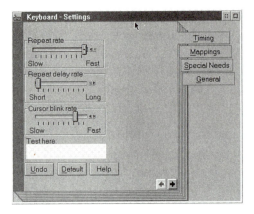

Figure 7.2 The Timing page of the Keyboard Settings notebook.

Timing

The Timing tab contains settings that control the speed of the cursor:

Repeat rate Determines the number of times per second a key repeats when you hold it down.

Repeat delay rate Determines how long the system waits to start repeating when you hold down a key.

Cursor blink rate Determines the blinking speed of the insertion point cursor.

Test here Click here to test the timing settings. Press and hold a key to test the delay and repeat rate. Observe the flashing cursor rate here as you change the blink rate setting.

Mappings

With the Mappings settings, you can remap the keys used to display object pop-up menus and the key/mouse combination used to change the title of an object.

Special Needs

You use the Special Needs settings to set up consecutive key assignments for key combinations. Consecutive key assignments let you press Ctrl, Alt, and Shift combinations by pressing one key at a time, instead of all at once.

General

You use the General tab to change the name of an object as well as to change the icon associated with an object. To change the name of an object, click in the Title area and type the new name. To change the icon, click on the Help button provided and follow the instructions listed there.

Changing the Mouse

Click on the Mouse object in the System Setup folder to change the way your mouse behaves. Figure 7.3 shows the settings screen.

Lesson 7

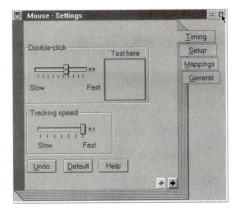

Figure 7.3 The Timing page of the Mouse Settings notebook.

Timing

The Timing tab contains settings that control the speed of the mouse response:

Double-click speed Use this setting to control how quickly you must double-click for OS/2 to distinguish between a double-click and two consecutive clicks. Double-click on the Test here box to test the double-click speed.

Tracking speed Use this setting to control how far and how quickly the mouse pointer moves when you move your mouse.

Setup

Use this setting to reverse the relative positions of mouse buttons 1 and 2 (that's why this book uses "button 1" and "button 2" instead of "left mouse button" and "right mouse button").

Mappings

Use this notebook settings page to determine which buttons are used for:

Dragging   The default is button 2.

Window list   The default is to click buttons 1 and 2 on the Desktop.

Displaying pop-up menus   The default is to click button 2 on the Desktop.

Editing title text   The default is Alt-button 1.

Switching Countries

Use country settings to change the way time, dates, measurements, money, and numbers are represented. When you change countries, OS/2 automatically uses preset defaults for Time, Dates, and Numbers. You can change any or all of the preset defaults.

Controlling Sound

Use the sound object to control whether or not OS/2 generates a warning beep for certain actions. This setting does not control all sound or all warning beeps—just the ones that OS/2 itself generates.

Lesson 7

Setting the System Clock

The System Clock displays the time and date. Use the clock settings (see Figure 7.4) to control the display (time, date, digital, analog, color, font, and so on), to set the system time and date, and to set an alarm. To open the Clock Settings notebook:

1. Open the System Clock by double-clicking on the System Clock object.

2. Click mouse button 2 on the Title Bar icon.

3. Click on the arrow to the right of the word **O**pen.

4. Click on Settings.

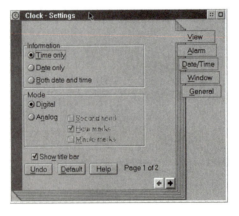

Figure 7.4   The Clock Settings notebook.

In this lesson, you learned how to control the way OS/2 behaves. In the next lesson, you'll learn how to control the way OS/2 looks.

Lesson 8
Controlling OS/2's Appearance

In this lesson, you will learn how to control the appearance of OS/2 using the Color, Scheme, and Font Palettes.

Using the Color Palette

Use the Color Palette to change screen colors of specific objects or of the entire system. To open the Color Palette, double-click on the Color Palette object in the System Setup folder. To change a color in an object:

1. Arrange the screen so that both the Color Palette and the object you want to change are visible on screen.

2. If necessary, use the Edit color button to put the colors you want on the palette.

3. Press and hold mouse button 2 while the pointer is positioned over the palette color circle you want to use, until a paint-roller icon appears.

4. Drag the paint roller to the part of the object you want to change (see Figure 8.1), and release the mouse button.

Lesson 8

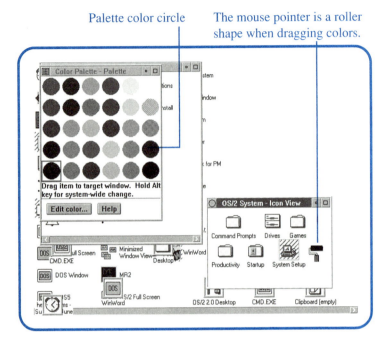

Figure 8.1 The Color Palette.

Paint the Whole Town Pink! To apply a color change to all objects of the same type, press and hold the Alt key before pressing mouse button 2 in step 3 above. For example, if you hold down the Alt key while you drag the paint roller to a window title bar, all title bars in all windows will change to the color you select.

It Won't Change! You cannot use the Color Palette object to change the colors of screen parts too small to accommodate the paint roller. To make finer color adjustments, use the Scheme Palette.

Using the Scheme Palette

Use the Scheme Palette to create color sets (schemes) and to make fine adjustments to screen colors. The Scheme Palette is a color and font template. First you change the template. When you're satisfied with the template, you then use the template to change an object's whole color scheme all at once.

What's a Template? A *template* is a model object that you can use to create or change other OS/2 objects. Just as you might use a pattern to shape a dress or a piece of furniture, you use a scheme template to specify colors and fonts. When you use a template to color an object, the object takes on the color scheme of the template.

Open the Scheme Palette from the System Setup menu. Using the Scheme Palette is a two-step process:

1. Edit a scheme to set the colors and fonts you want.

2. Drag the scheme to the object you want to change.

Editing an Existing Scheme

To change part of the current system scheme, select Default as the scheme to edit. To perform more sweeping changes, select the scheme closest to your preference and modify it. To leave the existing schemes intact, select one of the New Schemes to modify (renaming it as you like). To modify the selected scheme, click on the Edit scheme button to display the Edit Scheme window (see Figure 8.2).

Lesson 8

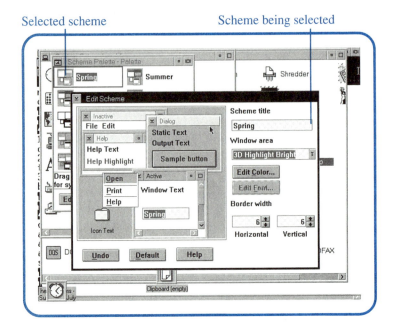

Figure 8.2 The Edit scheme window.

The boxed area in the left two-thirds of the screen displays the colors currently in effect and the names of the screen elements. To change an element in the selected scheme:

1. Select a window part from the Window Area list.

2. Select Edit Color or Edit Font, whichever applies.

3. Change the color or font to what you want.

4. Close the Edit Color or Edit Font window when you're done.

5. Close the Edit Scheme window.

Controlling OS/2's Appearance

6. Point the mouse to the scheme you just edited and press mouse button 2.

7. Drag the scheme icon to the window you want to change (hold down the Alt key to make the change systemwide).

Quick Switch with the Mouse In steps 1 through 3, you can select different window parts without closing the Edit Color or Edit Font window—just switch back and forth between the windows using the mouse.

Using the Font Palette

You can make some font changes using the Scheme Palette object. When you use the Scheme Palette to change fonts, you make changes to a scheme and then apply them all at once to an object or to the system. The Font Palette, on the other hand, acts directly on the fonts. Open the Font Palette from the System Setup folder to display the window shown in Figure 8.3.

Figure 8.3 The Font Palette.

51

Lesson 8

Limited Choices? The eight fonts displayed in Figure 8.3 are not the only fonts available. They're just the eight fonts that happen to be on the Font Palette at the moment. Use Edit font to create a palette that suits your needs.

To replace a palette font:

1. Click mouse button 1 on the font you want to replace.

2. Click mouse button 1 on the Edit font button.

3. Select the name, size, style, and emphasis you want to use.

4. Close the Edit font window.

To apply a selected font to a window or window part:

1. Drag the new font to the window or window part you want to change, using button 2.

2. Release the mouse button.

Adding and Deleting Fonts

You can use the font editor also to add and remove OS/2 fonts. To add fonts:

1. Put the disk containing the new fonts into floppy drive A.

2. Click on the Edit Fonts button.

3. Click on the Add button.

4. Click again on the Add button.

5. Click on each font file you want to add.

6. Click on the Add button.

To delete fonts you no longer want:

1. Click on the Edit fonts button.

2. Click on the Delete button.

3. Select each of the fonts you want to delete.

4. Click on the Delete button.

In this lesson, you learned how to redecorate OS/2. In the next lesson, you'll learn how to rearrange the furniture by organizing the Desktop.

Lesson 9

Organizing the Desktop

In this lesson, you'll learn how to organize or reorganize OS/2's Desktop to suit your needs. You'll learn how to add programs to folders, move objects around, and create copies of frequently needed objects in convenient locations.

Migrating Applications

Migration usually means to change from one operating environment to another. In OS/2, *migration* means to make programs available from the Workplace Shell. You do not have to migrate applications to use them, but doing so makes OS/2 much more convenient.

To use the migrate facility:

1. Open the Migrate Applications object from the System Setup folder.

2. Deselect the drive(s) you don't want searched (all are selected, by default).

3. Click mouse button 1 on the kind(s) of applications you want to add (DOS, Windows, OS/2).

4. Click mouse button 1 on the Find button. Usually, a limited list of applications appears.

5. Alternately click on the application(s) you want to add and click on the Add button.

6. Click on OK.

7. Deselect any applications you don't want to migrate.

8. Click on Migrate.

Is That All? By default, the Find button in step 4 lists just those applications that are in OS/2's on-line migration database. If Find does not list programs you want to add, click on Add Programs just after step 4.

The Migrate facility places applications with matches from the migration database into one of three folders: OS/2 Applications, DOS Applications, or Windows Applications. Migrate places other programs into folders called Additional OS/2 Applications, Additional DOS Applications, and Additional Windows Applications.

Using Templates to Create Objects

You can use the Templates folder to create objects. You can also use it to create folders (subdirectories), install programs into other folders, and create various kinds of documents. To use a template:

1. Point the mouse at the template icon you want to use.

2. Press and hold mouse button 2.

55

Lesson 9

3. While holding the button, drag the template to a target folder.

4. Release the mouse button.

If you're creating a folder or a data file, nothing further happens. If you drop a Printer template onto the Desktop, a Create Printer window appears. If you're creating a program, the program settings menu automatically appears.

Using Folders

Folders on the Desktop have special properties. They usually store *references* to program and data files rather than files themselves. You can use folders to organize your work however you like—generically (all number-crunching programs in a single folder, all word processing programs in another, and so on), by project (a special folder for each distinct project), or in any other way that suits your work style.

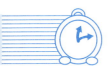

Open All At Once   One special kind of folder is a Work Area. When you close a Work Area, all open applications in that folder automatically close. When you open a Work Area, OS/2 restores all previously open applications (including window locations and sizes). To make a folder a Work Area, check the Work Area box (on the File tab of the Settings notebook).

Moving Objects Among Folders

You can rearrange OS/2 to put frequently needed objects directly on the Desktop. For example, you can move the command prompt icons directly into the Desktop folder. To move an object from one folder to another:

1. Open the folder that contains the object you want to move.

2. Open the destination folder.

3. Drag the object from the original location to the destination using mouse button 2.

Copying Objects

You can create copies of objects. To copy an object:

1. Open the folder containing the object.

2. Click mouse button 2 on the object.

3. Select the Copy option.

4. Select a target folder for the copy (this is where the copy will be placed).

5. Click on the Copy button.

Template Shortcut   If you just want to clone an object type (for example, create another program, but not another Lotus program), use the Create Another option instead of Copy. This usually is much quicker than using the Templates folder. Create Another creates a blank object of the same type, but does not copy the object's characteristics.

Copying versus Shadowing

A *shadow* is a linked duplicate of an object. When you change the original or any shadow, all other shadows and the original also change. To create a shadow:

1. Click mouse button 2 on the object you want to shadow.

2. Select a destination folder for the shadow.

3. Click on the Create button.

Using Selective Install

Use Selective Install, in the System Setup folder, to selectively install or reinstall any OS/2 components (CD-ROM, documentation, fonts, system utilities, tools, games, and so on). You also can use Selective Install to change your display adapter, mouse, or keyboard.

Using Device Driver Install

Use Device Driver Install, located in the System Setup folder, to install device drivers (for example, CD-ROMs or display adapters) that come on diskettes. For the process to work, the device driver diskette must contain a profile control file. Follow the instructions specific to the device driver you are installing. Different procedures vary widely.

Profile Control File This is a set of instructions written by programmers that tell how a specific device driver is installed. Profile control files are put onto device driver diskettes by whoever provides the device driver diskette. Such diskettes are sometimes provided with display adaptors, hard disk controllers, CD-ROM controllers, or other hardware you add to your computer system.

In this lesson, you learned how to use folders to organize your work. Next, you'll learn about OS/2 file systems.

Lesson 10

Understanding OS/2 File Systems

In this lesson, you'll learn the essentials of OS/2 file systems. You'll learn the differences between HPFS and FAT, and the advantages and disadvantages of each.

What Is a File System?

A file system is a way of organizing data on your disk. PC DOS and MS-DOS both use something called a FAT (File Allocation Table) system. OS/2, on the other hand, uses both FAT and HPFS (High Performance File System).

A file system organizes programs and data on a disk into directories—each directory, each distinct program, and each distinct set of data (including documents) is stored as a file. The HPFS tends to be faster than FAT because files are stored in larger areas on disk, and because the method for finding a file on disk is more efficient.

So, why offer FAT at all? It's the only file system that works on floppy disks—for now. It's also a convenient way for users to have both OS/2 and DOS on the same computer. It's a way for OS/2 to offer backward compatibility without being backward itself.

Understanding HPFS and FAT

The most important practical differences between HPFS and FAT are shown in Table 10.1.

Table 10.1 FAT versus HPFS.

Pro	Con
FAT	
FAT is required for all floppy disks	Limited to "old-fashioned" 8.3 file names
Requires less memory than HPFS	Slower access than HPFS on most OS/2 systems
Compatible with both DOS and OS/2	Prone to file fragmentation
HPFS	
Allows file names up to 254 characters	Can't be read by real DOS
Faster access than FAT on most disks	Requires an additional 500K of memory
Can be read by OS/2's DOS and WIN-OS/2	File system errors can be difficult to deal with
Resists fragmentation	Requires reformatting the disk

File Fragmentation A file system can store a file in one contiguous section of a disk, or in several distinct areas—the latter is called *fragmentation*. A fragmented file is more subject to file errors, and takes longer to access.

Finding Out If You Can Use HPFS

If your computer system has limited memory (generally 4M or less), using HPFS probably will not improve overall performance. The extra memory required for HPFS means more swapping to disk, greatly reducing any HPFS speed advantage. Also, if the disk is less than 65M, HPFS advantages tend to be much lower.

If you have 8M or more of memory, and if you have a hard disk larger than 65M, you will definitely benefit from HPFS. All programs running under OS/2 can use HPFS partitions—including your DOS and Windows programs. The benefits are better file integrity and faster performance. Disk-intensive programs such as database and spreadsheet programs—even the DOS and Windows versions—usually run much more quickly on HPFS than on FAT. Only real DOS in a non-OS/2 system cannot read from HPFS.

What Are Extended Attributes?

For both HPFS and FAT file systems, OS/2 uses something called Extended Attributes (EA). An *attribute* is a piece of information about a file. In DOS and OS/2, a file's attributes include the date and time of last update, as well as read-only, archive, system, and hidden status.

EAs comprise information beyond the normal DOS-style attributes. EAs can include whatever information a programmer wants to include—the name and location of associated icons, the name of the program that created the file, additional dates and times relevant to the file, and so on. OS/2 and OS/2 programs also use EAs to store object settings and preferences. Using EAs means that programs start more quickly, and are better at remembering what you do from session to session.

Where Are the EAs on a FAT Disk?

In a FAT system, EAs are stored in hidden files, named EA DATA.SF, on each disk partition. When you use a Drive object to copy OS/2 files to a floppy disk, EA DATA.SF is created or updated on the receiving floppy disk. In an HPFS partition, EAs are attached to files, and no EA DATA.SF file is used.

What's a Partition? A *partition* is a fixed area on a hard disk that's used to store a file system. A hard disk can contain a single partition or several partitions, depending on how you want to use it. You use the FDISK command to create, delete, and change partitions on a hard disk.

Naming Files—Dos and Don'ts

File naming conventions in OS/2 are similar to those in DOS. For both HPFS and FAT disks:

1. A file name can't use illegal characters. These are:

    - ASCII characters 0 through 31
    - " / \ : ? | < > - &
    - @ as the first character of a program name

2. A file name must contain at least one character.

3. A file name cannot be a reserved name. The following names are reserved by OS/2:

COM1	COM2	COM3
LPT1	LPT2	LPT3
NUL	PRN	CLOCK$
CON	SCREEN$	POINTER$
MOUSE$	KBD	

Under FAT, a file name can have only eight characters as the name, and up to three characters as the file extension. You must separate the two parts with a period. This format sometimes is called *8.3* format.

HPFS file names can be up to 254 characters, and can include any number of periods and spaces. HPFS file names also retain case information, although upper- and lowercase versions of any given file name are identical (for example, "ThisName" is the same file name as "THISNAME" and "thisname").

Where's My File? HPFS file names that do not meet FAT specifications are invisible to programs that are not HPFS-aware, even when running under OS/2. HPFS-unaware programs include DOS and Windows programs, as well as a number of OS/2 version 1 programs. If a file does not show up in a program's file listing, use a Drive object (see Lesson 11) or the OS/2 command line (see Lesson 15) to verify that the file exists. Enhanced HPFS file names are also invisible when using OS/2 emulation of DOS and Windows.

In this lesson, you learned about OS/2 file systems, as well as the advantages of HPFS. Next, you'll learn how to look at your file system using OS/2's innovative drive objects.

Lesson 11
Displaying Directories with Drive Objects

In this lesson, you will learn how to use drive objects to display directories and files and to format a diskette.

What Is a Drive Object?

OS/2's object-oriented approach to file management uses drive objects. You can use drive objects to copy, view, move, delete, and rename files and directories (folders). You can also use drive objects to format diskettes and to execute programs.

Let's Get Organized *File management* refers to how you organize your files. When you create a subdirectory and move files to it—that's file management. When you delete surplus backup or temporary files you no longer need—that's file management.

To open the Drives folder:

- Double-click mouse button 1 on Drives in the OS/2 System Folder.

65

Lesson 11

The first view of the Drives folder shows all available drives recognized by OS/2 (see Figure 11.1).

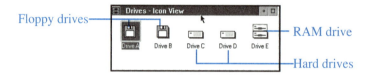

Figure 11.1   The Drives folder.

The icon used for each type of drive is different. A and B are floppy drives, C and D are hard drives, and E is a RAM (virtual) drive. To open a specific drive:

- Double-click mouse button 1 on the drive's icon.

Don't Drive Empty!   When opening a floppy drive object, make sure that the drive contains a diskette. Otherwise, you'll get the scary SYS0039 error message. The message is harmless. Just insert a diskette and select the Retry option.

Displaying a Tree View

When you open a drive, the default view is Tree view, as shown in Figure 11.2. The Tree view shows only the organizational structures (folders or directories). The Tree view is useful for general navigation and overall directory management, but not for running programs and working with files.

66

Displaying Directories with Drive Objects

The minus sign indicates that a subfolder is displayed.

The plus sign indicates that this folder contains subfolders.

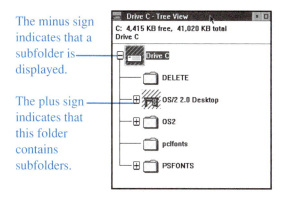

Figure 11.2 A Tree view of drive C.

Displaying an Icon View

To see an icon view of a drive's root directory:

- Double-click on the Drive icon in the tree diagram. You'll see a window like that shown in Figure 11.3.

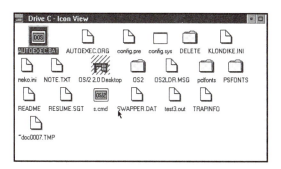

Figure 11.3 An Icon view of a hard disk directory.

67

Lesson 11

In Icon view, you can:

- Run any program by double-clicking on its icon.
- Open an Icon view of any folder.
- Open any data file to edit it by double-clicking on its icon.
- Rename any object by selecting its object pop-up menu.
- Copy, delete, and move files.

See Lessons 12 and 13 for additional information.

Displaying a Details View

If you migrated to OS/2 from DOS, you undoubtedly are more accustomed to seeing the directory view you get from typing DIR at the command line. The Icon view is OS/2's default view. To see the more DOS-like Details view:

1. Use a Drive object to navigate to the subdirectory you want to see.
2. Click mouse button 2 on the folder you want to see, to display the object pop-up menu.
3. Click on the arrow to the right of the word **O**pen.
4. Click on Details view to see the window shown in Figure 11.4.

   The Details view provides the following information:

- Real name
- File title

Displaying Directories with Drive Objects

- File size
- Last write date and time
- Last access date and time
- Creation date and time
- Attribute flags (Archive, System, Hidden, Read-only)

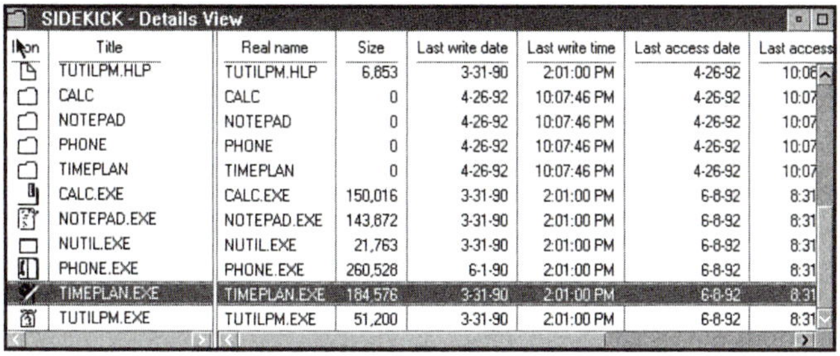

Figure 11.4 An OS/2 directory in Details view.

The entire Details view does not fit on an ordinary VGA screen. Use the scroll bars to see additional information.

Formatting Diskettes with a Drive Object

To format a diskette:

1. Insert the diskette into the drive.
2. Click mouse button 2 on the drive object that contains the diskette.
3. Click on Format disk.

69

Lesson 11

4. If a SYS0039 pop-up error message appears, select Return Error Code, and then click on OK.

5. When the Format window appears, type a volume label. (The volume label is optional—you can leave it blank if you want.)

6. Select the capacity for the disk.

7. Click on Format.

8. When finished, click on OK.

9. Click on Format to format another diskette, or Cancel to stop.

What's a Volume Label? It's an optional name that lets you know what's on a disk. A useful volume label might be EXPENSES or BACKUP0001. Volume labels may be up to 11 characters long. When you use the command line DIR command on a floppy disk, its volume label is displayed at the top of the directory listing, letting you see at a glance what the disk contains.

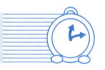

Work While Formatting After you click on Format, you can continue working in other windows. Open the Window list and switch to the task you want to continue while the diskette is still being formatted. When disk activity stops, press Alt-Esc to cycle back to the Format window.

In this lesson, you learned how to view directories and format diskettes using a drive object. In the next lesson, you will learn how to use drive objects to copy files and folders.

Lesson 12

Copying Files and Folders with the Drive Object

In this lesson, you will learn how to copy files and folders using drive objects.

Copying from HPFS to FAT

To copy from an OS/2 directory to a FAT drive (for example, to copy from a hard disk to a floppy disk):

1. Open the drive object for the file(s) or folder(s) you want to copy.

2. To select each object you want to copy, hold down the Ctrl key and click mouse button 1.

3. Click mouse button 2 on any selected object to pop up the common object menu for all selected objects.

4. Select the Copy option.

5. Click on the Drives tab (see Figure 12.1).

6. If the target drive is a floppy, make sure that it contains a formatted disk.

7. Double-click on the destination drive.

Lesson 12

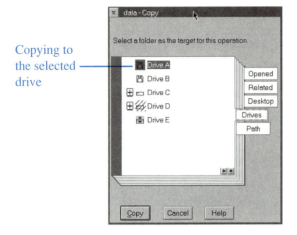

Copying to the selected drive

Figure 12.1 Copying files from a hard drive to a floppy drive.

This will copy any selected files and subdirectories (including any files within those subdirectories) to the target drive. It also updates the receiving disk's EA to reflect the file transfer. If you use enhanced file names, the names are shortened on the target FAT drive, and any spaces are converted into underscore characters (_). However, the original longer name is stored in the EA file, and will be preserved when you use the drive's object to recopy the files to an HPFS drive.

What Happened to My Extended Attributes?
To preserve EAs and long file names when copying files from HPFS to floppy, you must use a drive object. The COPY command, when executed from the OS/2 command line, copies just the file, stripping out the extended attributes. The Copy option in a drive object, however, preserves attributes by creating and/or updating EA DATA.SF on the target drive.

72

Copying Files and Folders with the Drive Object

Copying from Folder to Folder

When copying from folder to folder, it's useful to open all folders involved. To copy from one folder to another:

1. Open the drive objects for the folders you want to use. (See Figure 12.2.)

2. Open the folders that contain the files or folders you want to copy.

3. Select the files or folders you want to copy.

4. Click mouse button 2 on any of the selected objects.

5. Click on the target directory to select a destination.

6. Click on the Copy button to begin copying.

   Alternatively, you can combine steps 5 and 6 by double-clicking on the target directory.

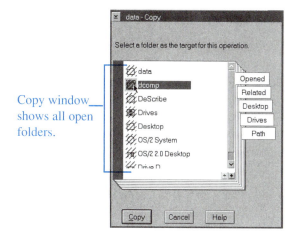

Copy window shows all open folders.

Figure 12.2 Copying between folders on the same drive.

73

Lesson 12

Keyboard + Mouse = Shortcut   For faster copying when source and target folders both are open, you can drag objects from folder to folder. Ordinarily, dragging moves rather than copies objects. Press and hold the Ctrl key while dragging the selected objects, and OS/2 will copy them to the target folder.

In this lesson, you learned how and why to use drive objects for copying files. In the next lesson, you learn some of the drive object's other tricks—moving, deleting, renaming, and creating files and folders.

Lesson 13

Managing Files and Folders with the Drive Object

In this lesson, you'll learn how to move, delete, undelete, rename, and create objects.

Moving Objects

To move objects (for example, files and folders) across hard disk folders (directories):

1. Open the drive objects for the source and target folders.

2. Select the files or subfolders you want to move.

3. Point to any selected object, and press and hold mouse button 2.

4. Drag the selected object(s) to the target, as shown in Figure 13.1, and release the mouse button.

If the operation involves a floppy disk drive, dragging does not move the objects; it copies them. If the operation involves two different partitions on a hard drive (even if they're on different physical drives), dragging copies the files to the destination, and deletes them at the source.

Lesson 13

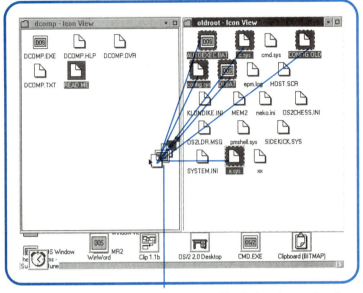

Mouse pointer shows a series of selected files being dragged to the DCOMP folder.

Figure 13.1 Dragging files across directories or folders.

Deleting Objects

You can delete files and folders by either dragging them to the Shredder or using the Delete option from an object's pop-up menu. To delete an object when both the object and the Shredder are visible:

1. Use mouse button 2 to drag the object to the Shredder.

2. Release the mouse button.

3. If prompted, confirm the deletion.

If the deleted object is a folder, OS/2 will prompt you to confirm before deleting folders and their contents.

Folders Are Shreddable There are several different kinds of folders—some contain files and some don't. When working with a drives object, the folders you see usually correspond to subdirectories, and contain files. If you delete a subdirectory, all files it contains are deleted. If you do accidentally delete a subdirectory full of files, and if you have UNDELETE enabled, you may be able to get back some or all of your files. From the OS/2 command line (see Lesson 14), use the MKDIR command to re-create the subdirectory, and then run UNDELETE to see what can be recovered.

Undeleting Files

If enabled, OS/2 provides the capability to undelete files you've deleted. Unfortunately, there is no object-oriented method built into OS/2 for undeleting files as yet. To enable UNDELETE, you must edit your CONFIG.SYS file. First, make a backup copy of CONFIG.SYS. To edit CONFIG.SYS:

1. Open the OS/2 System Editor (see Lesson 18 for more on editing text).

2. Select **File Open**, and select CONFIG.SYS from C:\.

3. Find the line that looks like the following:

   ```
   REM SET DELDIR=C:\DELETE,512;
   ```

Lesson 13

4. Remove the REM by placing the cursor at the beginning of the line and pressing the Delete key four times (be sure to remove the space after the M).

5. Select File Save.

6. If prompted, set the Type to OS/2 Command File, and click on Set.

7. Double-click OS/2 System Editor's Title Bar icon to close the Editor.

8. Close all open applications (programs).

9. Display the Desktop pop-up menu, and Shut down the system.

10. Press Ctrl-Alt-Delete to reboot your computer.

To enable UNDELETE in DOS sessions, you must place the identical line into your AUTOEXEC.BAT file, as well.

UNDELETE works only from the command line. To undelete a file:

1. Open the OS/2 Command Prompt from the Command Prompts folder (which is in the OS/2 System folder).

2. Type `UNDELETE disk:\path\filename.ext` (for example, type `UNDELETE C:\DATA\MYFILE.DAT`).

3. Type Y to confirm the undelete.

See Lessons 14 and 15 to learn how to open and use the OS/2 command line.

When you delete a file, a hidden copy of it goes into the DELETE folder. When a deletion would make the size of the DELETE folder go above the maximum space allotted (512K is the default set in step 3 above, editing the CONFIG. SYS file), OS/2 permanently deletes files from the DELETE folder to make room (first in, first out).

Renaming Objects

To rename an object:

1. Display the object's Settings pop-up menu.

2. Select the General tab.

3. Type the new name in the Title field.

4. Double-click on the Settings Title Bar icon to close.

If the object icon is visible on-screen in a folder or in the window list, a quicker way to change its title is:

1. Press and hold the Alt key and click mouse button 1 on the name you want to change; this opens the name field for editing, as shown in Figure 13.2.

2. Type the new name.

3. Click anywhere else in the current window.

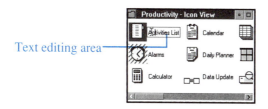

Figure 13.2 Changing an object's name directly in a folder.

Lesson 13

Creating Subdirectories

In OS/2, a subdirectory is a folder that holds files. To create a subdirectory:

- Drag a folder template from the Template folder to the folder where you want to create a subdirectory.

You can also use an existing directory (folder) as a template:

1. Open the target Drive object.

2. Open folders until you're in the target directory.

3. Click mouse button 2 on any existing directory.

4. Click on the Create another menu option (see Figure 13.3).

5. Double-click on the destination directory.

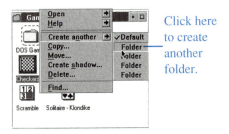

Figure 13.3 Using an existing folder as a template.

In this lesson, you learned how to move, delete, rename, create, and undelete files and folders. In the next lesson, you'll learn how to open and close OS/2 command line sessions.

Lesson 14
Finding the OS/2 Command Prompt

In this lesson, you will learn how to open and close one or more OS/2 command prompt sessions.

Command Line versus Object Orientation

One of the main goals of OS/2's object-oriented graphical user interface is to minimize the time you spend at the command line. While OS/2's object orientation may be ideal for the newcomer who doesn't have any DOS experience, it can be cumbersome to command-line veterans.

At Your Command A *command line*, also called a *command prompt* or the *C prompt*, is the most basic way of controlling OS/2 or DOS. It usually looks like this: C:\os2>, where C:\os2 is the current disk and directory. A command prompt is OS/2's way of saying "I'm ready to do something—tell me what to do!" In order to control OS/2 from the command prompt, you type commands. For example, type **DIR** to show a listing of files and directories.

Lesson 14

Opening an OS/2 Command Line Session

To access the OS/2 command line:

1. Open the OS/2 System folder.

2. Open the Command Prompts folder.

3. Double-click on either OS/2 Full Screen or OS/2 Window.

For most purposes, the OS/2 Window is superior to Full Screen. Here are several reasons why:

- It offers adjustable window and font sizes.

- It allows you to cut and paste using the clipboard.

- It provides mouse support.

- It provides a scrollable buffer (up to 102 lines).

Why Doesn't It Switch? In a DOS command window, you can press Alt-Home to toggle between windowed and full-screen command lines. The same trick does not work in an OS/2 window. OS/2 windowed and full-screen sessions are quite different from one another—you can't toggle them. If you need the benefits of the Clipboard, you must run OS/2 in a window right from the start.

Finding the OS/2 Command Prompt

Closing an OS/2 Command Line Session

To close an OS/2 command line session:

- Type `exit` and press Enter.

You also can close a windowed OS/2 command line session by pressing Alt followed by C, or by double-clicking the Title Bar icon. When you go that route, OS/2 prompts you to confirm closing the window. The Exit method is cleaner and quicker.

Don't Kill That Window! Don't use the Alt, C or Title Bar icon methods to close an open OS/2 window when a program is still running in it. Most programs have built-in methods for terminating safely—use the built-in method whenever possible. Use the Alt, C and Title Bar icon methods only when necessary to close a hung program. Failure to exit a program properly can lose data and corrupt files.

Opening Multiple OS/2 Command Line Sessions

By default, if you double-click on a command prompt object in a folder when a command line session of that type is already open, OS/2 switches to the already-open session. If you want multiple command prompts instead, you can change the way that the Open command works.

83

Lesson 14

To change the behavior of the command line object's **O**pen command:

1. Click mouse button 2 on the command prompt object you want to change.

2. Click mouse button 1 on the arrow to the right of **O**pen.

3. Click mouse button 1 on the Settings option.

4. Click mouse button 1 on the Window tab to reveal the settings screen shown in Figure 14.1.

5. Select Create new window under Object open behavior.

6. Double-click mouse button 1 on the Title Bar icon to close the Settings panel.

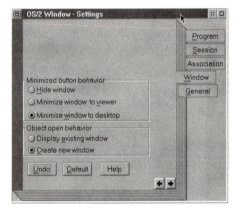

Figure 14.1 Changing object open behavior.

In this lesson, you learned how to open and close OS/2 command line sessions. In the next lesson, you'll learn how to use the OS/2 command line.

Lesson 15
Using the OS/2 Command Line

In this lesson, you will learn how to run programs from the OS/2 command line, how to edit command-line input, and how to summon help.

The OS/2 Command Line

For the most part, the OS/2 command line works very much like the DOS command line. Normal commands like COPY, DIR, TYPE, and DEL work nearly identically to their DOS counterparts. Furthermore, OS/2 provides additional commands, including START and DETACH, that enable multitasking from a single command line. See the command reference at the end of this book for more about START, DETACH, and other OS/2 commands.

Running Programs

To run a program from the command line, you just type its name followed by any parameters needed—just as you would when running DOS. For example, to edit AUTOEXEC.BAT from the command line using the E.EXE editor, change to the appropriate directory and type:

Lesson 15

```
e autoexec.bat
```

What's Happening? You can run DOS, Windows or OS/2 programs from the OS/2 command line. Depending on the kind of program, OS/2 may do some strange-looking things before the program finally appears on your screen. It may appear convulsive. Don't worry. OS/2 is just loading the resources it needs to run the program. If the program is a character-based OS/2 program, OS/2 runs it without hesitation. For any other type of program—DOS, Windows, or Presentation Manager (PM)—OS/2 switches screen modes and loads the appropriate environment.

Using Enhanced Filenames

Most common filing commands work the same under OS/2 as in DOS. If you use enhanced filenames that contain spaces, however, you must enclose the name in quotes. For example, to log to the OS!2 2.0 Desktop directory, use:

```
CD "OS!2 2.0 Desktop"
```

Similarly, when copying, deleting, moving, and so on, you must enclose the whole name in quotes. File names without spaces do not require quotes.

Editing the Command Line

The OS/2 command line has a command stack, but does not have an equivalent to DOSKEY's aliasing ability for frequently used commands. DOSKEY is available in OS/2's DOS sessions, but not at the OS/2 command line.

DOSKEY is a DOS program that makes it possible to use ↑ and ↓ to redisplay previously typed commands at the command line. DOSKEY also enables you to easily change a previously issued command and reissue the command. The list of all commands you have typed during a session is called the *command stack*. When you press ↑, the previous command is displayed on the command line. If you press ↑ again, the command prior to that one is displayed. Use ↓ to cycle the commands in the opposite direction. When the most recent command is displayed, ↓ displays the least recent command in the stack. The next press displays the next least recent command. DOSKEY also enables *aliasing*.

The KEYS to Success! The KEYS command is similar to DOSKEY. KEYS can be turned on in CONFIG.SYS or at the OS/2 command line. In CONFIG.SYS, the line SET KEYS=ON enables the OS/2 command stack and command line editing. KEYS does not have an aliasing capability. At the OS/2 command line, you can turn KEYS on or off by typing KEYS mode, where mode is OFF or ON.

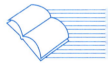

What's Aliasing? An *alias* is a shorthand for a longer command or hard-to-remember command. For example, CDDESK might be an alias for CD "OS!2 2.0 Desktop".

Using the Command Stack

With KEYS ON (the OS/2 default set in CONFIG.SYS), the OS/2 command line provides a command stack that you

can use to retrieve previously entered commands from the current session. To use the command stack, press ↑ and ↓ to cycle through up to 64K worth of previously entered commands. To see a list of all commands in the stack, type:

KEYS LIST

Editing Modes

The OS/2 command line has two editing modes:

- KEYS ON

- KEYS OFF

KEYS ON provides a command stack, but the function keys do not work as they do in DOS. With KEYS OFF, there is no command stack, but command-line editing works similarly to the way it works in DOS without DOSKEYS. The editing keys used with KEYS OFF are shown in Table 15.1.

With KEYS ON, editing keys are the same except that the function keys are disabled, and ← and → move the insertion point without affecting the command itself.

Getting Help

There are two kinds of command-line help, both of which use the HELP command. You can request help for a specific command at any time by typing **HELP** followed by the command name. For example, the command **HELP XCOPY** opens the OS/2 Command Reference to the section on the XCOPY command.

Table 15.1 Command-line editing keys used with KEYS OFF.

Key	Description
F1	Displays the previous command one character at a time.
F2	Displays part of the previous command up to the character you type.
F3	Displays the previous command.
F4	Deletes the first part of your previous command up to a letter you specify.
F6	Ctrl-Z (ASCII 26, the end-of-file character).
←	Deletes the character to the left of the cursor.
→	Undeletes the character to the right of the cursor (only after you press F3 or F1).
Backspace	Deletes the character to the left of the cursor.
Del	Deletes the character at the cursor.
Ins	Toggles between insert and overstrike modes.
Esc	Cancels the current command line.

When running OS/2, you may occasionally receive an error message. For example, if you double-click on the Drive A icon without putting a disk in drive A, the system will generate a SYS0039 error number. To see more information about SYS error numbers:

1. Open an OS/2 command prompt.

2. Type HELP *sysnumber* (for example, type HELP 39).

OS/2 will display a longer explanation of the error message along with possible causes and cures.

Lesson 15

In this lesson, you learned the basics of running programs from the OS/2 command line. In the next lesson, you'll learn about printing in OS/2.

Lesson 16
Printing in OS/2

In this lesson, you will learn about OS/2 printing, the Spooler, and how to add fonts to OS/2.

OS/2 Print Interface

OS/2 installs printer support for OS/2 applications. It indirectly installs support for Windows applications, too, through the Adobe Type Manager (ATM) for Windows (see Lesson 23). By using the same printer interface, all Presentation Manager (PM) and Windows applications have access to the same printer and capabilities.

Where's the FAX? If you install special printer drivers under WIN-OS/2—such as WinFax or Intel FAXability—they will not be available from PM applications. Similarly, if you install drivers under OS/2, they won't show up in WIN-OS/2. While ATM for Windows provides WIN-OS/2 the same font set that OS/2 has, WIN-OS/2 and OS/2 do not share the same printer drivers.

Lesson 16

Printing from Applications

Most applications that use the printer have a Print option, usually located in the File menu. To print from an application, choose its own Print option and follow the directions for the application you're using.

Printing Using Drag and Drop

You can print some, but not all, documents directly with drag and drop. Likely candidates are plain text files and printer-ready files (files that contain all of the necessary printer codes). To print using the drag-and-drop method:

1. Open the folder or drive object that contains the file you want to print.

2. Using mouse button 2, drag the file to the printer object.

3. Drop the file into the printer object by releasing the mouse button; this causes the window in Figure 16.1 to appear.

4. Select Plain Text if the file is just plain numbers and letters, with no embedded printer codes. Select Printer-specific if the file contains special codes.

It's a Gusher! Some files—like word processing documents, spreadsheet files, and .TIF and .PCX files—require an application to print correctly. If you drop one of those documents directly into a printer object, you may find your printer suddenly spews page after wasted page containing just a few characters. When that happens, open the Printer object and delete the misbehaving print job.

Printing in OS/2

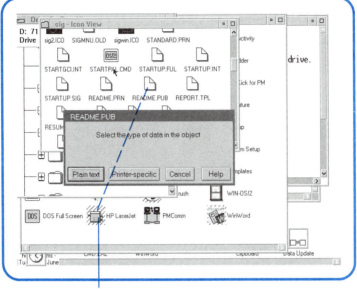

README.PUB was dragged and dropped onto the HP LaserJet printer object.

Figure 16.1 Using drag and drop to print.

Understanding Printers and Spoolers

Users sometimes confuse the printer with the Spooler. The printer is the hardware device on which you print. Each printer has an associated print queue (a waiting list for print jobs). The OS/2 Spooler is a software device that acts like a traffic cop for print queues. The idea is to let the application print at top speed to the spool file, and then let the Spooler take over. The OS/2 Spooler controls all printing sent to the default printer port—OS/2, WIN-OS/2, and DOS—providing faster and safer printing.

93

Setting the Spooler Location

You set the Spooler file location with the Spooler settings panel. By default, OS/2 installs the Spooler on the OS/2 system disk, usually C:\SPOOL. Depending on your printing needs, this location might not provide enough disk space. Make sure the location you specify has enough free space to accommodate large spool files. To specify a spool location:

1. Double-click on the Spooler in the OS/2 System Setup folder.

2. Type a disk and path for the Spooler.

3. Close the Spooler by double-clicking the Title Bar icon.

Disabling the Spooler

If you are concerned about security, you might sometimes decide not to use the Spooler, since others can examine the spool file while it is waiting to be printed. To disable the Spooler:

1. Click mouse button 2 on the Spooler icon in the System Setup folder.

2. Click on the Disable Spooler option.

3. Click on the OK button—a message reminds you to shut down your system.

4. Shut down and restart your system.

Printing in OS/2

Enabling the Spooler

The Disable Spooler option acts as a toggle. To re-enable the Spooler after you have disabled it:

1. Click mouse button 2 on the Spooler icon.

2. Click either button on the Enable Spooler option.

   When you enable the Spooler, you do not have to restart your system—OS/2 activates the Spooler immediately.

Adding Printer Fonts

Printer fonts for the OS/2 printer come from two sources:

- Built-in Adobe Type I fonts.

- Additional fonts provided by the user (cartridge or soft fonts).

Most applications that print formatted text provide options that show the available fonts. To add Adobe Type I fonts:

1. Select the Font Palette from the System Setup folder.

2. Click on Edit fonts.

3. Click on Add.

4. Type the source location of the fonts you want to add (or accept A:).

5. Click on Add.

6. Select each font you want to add.

7. Click on Add.

You can use the printer object to add or change soft fonts and font cartridges. To add soft fonts or change font cartridges:

1. Open the Settings notebook for the printer object.

2. Click on Printer Driver.

3. Click mouse button 2 on the default printer driver (see Figure 16.2).

4. Click on the arrow to the right of Open.

5. Click on Settings.

6. Select the cartridge(s) you have from the list.

7. To add fonts, click on Fonts.

8. Select the correct source device, and click on Open.

9. Select the fonts you want to add.

10. Click on Add.

11. Close the Settings notebook.

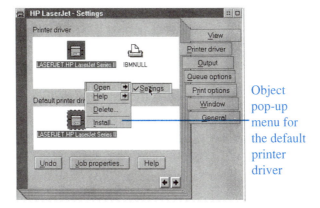

Figure 16.2 Accessing the default printer driver's settings.

In this lesson, you learned the basics of printing in OS/2. In the next lesson, you'll learn how to manage jobs sent to the printer.

Lesson 17
Managing Print Jobs

In this lesson, you will learn how OS/2 manages print jobs, how to change the order of print jobs, and how to change printer characteristics.

Print Jobs

Unless you disable the spooler, OS/2 automatically manages your print jobs for you. OS/2 directs all printing to a specific printer object into its queue. When you print to a printer object, the printer driver sends the print job to the appropriate subdirectory (print queue). From there, the spooler takes over and sends the jobs to the printer. The spooler regulates the flow of output to the printer so that different print jobs don't overprint each other.

 **Think Queue** A *print queue* is simply a subdirectory. If you have three printer objects set up, your spooler directory will contain one subdirectory for queuing each printer object's output.

Using the Printer Object

You can use the printer object to change settings and to view and change the status of jobs in the print queue. To put all printing for a given printer object on hold:

1. Click mouse button 2 on the printer object.

2. Click on Change status.

3. Click on Hold.

   To view all printing jobs in the current queue, open the printer object. To see a more informative view of what's happening, select the Details view:

1. Click mouse button 2 on the printer object.

2. Click on the arrow to the right of Open.

3. Click on Details view (see Figure 17.1).

Reordering Printing

If your print queue becomes especially full, you can change the priority of print jobs. To do this, you put all jobs not printing on hold, and then release them for printing in the order you prefer. To change print order:

1. Open the printer object.

2. Press Ctrl-/ to select all of the listed print jobs.

3. Point the mouse at any selected print job and click mouse button 2.

4. Select the Change status option.

Lesson 17

5. Click on Hold.

6. Press Ctrl-\ to deselect all of the print jobs.

7. One at a time, select and release jobs in the order you want them printed.

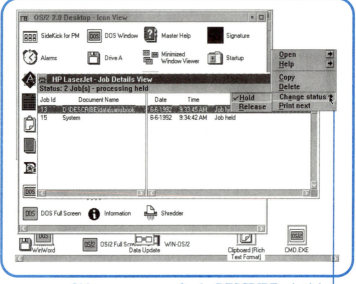

Object pop-up menu for the DESCRIBE print job

Figure 17.1   Displaying print jobs in the queue.

It Won't Stop!   You cannot use the Status option to hold a print job once it's actually started printing. Once printing has started, your best option is to switch your printer off-line. Once the printer's buffer is empty, OS/2 will be unable to send more data to the printer. OS/2 then gives you the `Printer is not Responding` message, offering you the choice of **A**bort, **R**etry, or **I**gnore. Select Abort to cancel the print job.

Managing Print Jobs

Changing Printer Characteristics

You also use the printer object to change certain aspects of the printer. To change the printer:

1. Click mouse button 2 on the printer object.

2. Click on the arrow next to the word **O**pen.

3. Click on Settings.

This reveals the settings notebook window shown in Figure 17.2.

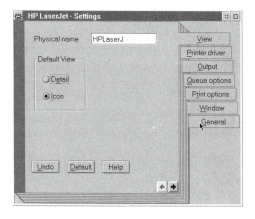

Figure 17.2 Using the printer settings notebook.

The settings notebook lets you make changes to the following:

View   Lets you switch between Icon or Detail view.

Printer driver   Lets you select among installed drivers.

Lesson 17

Output Lets you select the printing port, or lets you direct output to a file.

Queue options Lets you select queue options.

Print options Lets you specify a separator file to go between print jobs; also lets you set a time range during which printing is performed.

Window Lets you control how the printer object is displayed.

General Lets you rename the printer object and change the icon associated with it.

You can also use the Printer Driver page of the settings notebook to manage a variety of printer settings, including font cartridges, device defaults (paper tray, orientation, and so on), and soft fonts. To manipulate device defaults directly, you can select the Job Properties button from the Printer driver page. You will see the window shown in Figure 17.3.

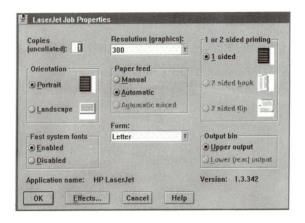

Figure 17.3   The Job Properties menu.

102

Managing Print Jobs

To change other aspects of the printer driver, use the printer driver settings menu. To change printer driver settings:

1. Click mouse button 2 on the default printer driver.

2. Click on the arrow to the right of the word **O**pen.

3. Click on Settings. You will see the window shown in Figure 17.4.

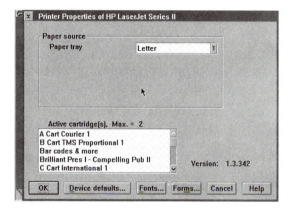

Figure 17.4   The default printer driver settings.

The **F**onts button lets you change, add, and delete fonts. The **D**evice defaults menu is the same menu you see when you select Job Properties from the **P**rinter driver tab in the Printer object menu. The For**m**s button lets you assign your own names to predefined form (paper) sizes.

In this lesson, you learned how to control printing and how to change printer settings. In the next three lessons, you'll learn about OS/2's built-in applications, starting with the System Editor.

Lesson 18
Editing Text

In this lesson, you'll learn how to use the System Editor. You'll also learn when not to use the Enhanced File Editor.

OS/2 Editors

Basic editing techniques—moving the insertion point, selecting text, inserting and deleting, and using the Clipboard—are common across most OS/2 Presentation Manager (PM) and Windows applications. Use the techniques taught in this lesson whenever editing text in OS/2.

OS/2 provides two built-in editors:

System Editor   Suitable for editing text-only files, such as .CMD files, CONFIG.SYS, AUTOEXEC.BAT.

Enhanced File Editor   Suitable for files that require formatting and printing.

Editing Text

Using the System Editor

Use the System Editor to create and edit plain text files, system files (AUTOEXEC.BAT and CONFIG.SYS), and command files. The System Editor does not provide formatting or printing capabilities. If you need formatting and printing, use the Enhanced File Editor or a dedicated word processor.

To open the OS/2 System Editor:

1. Open the Productivity folder.

2. Double-click mouse button 1 on the OS/2 System Editor object icon. You will see the screen shown in Figure 18.1.

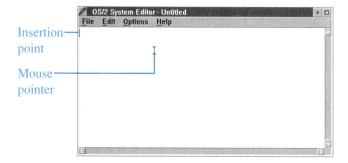

Figure 18.1 The System Editor main editing screen.

Editing Files

Use the System Editor to create new files or to modify existing files. To create a new file, double-click on the

105

OS/2 system editor object icon and just start typing. To edit an existing file:

1. Select File Open.

2. Select the drive and directory where the file is located.

3. Double-click mouse button 1 on the file you want to edit.

4. Alternatively, type the complete path name (for example, type `C:\AUTOEXEC.BAT`) after step 1.

Moving the Insertion Point

The insertion point shows where new text appears when you type. You can move the insertion point to any location in the text by pointing the mouse and clicking button 1. The mouse pointer is indicated by an I-beam. Other ways to move the insertion point are shown in Table 18.1.

Table 18.1 Moving the insertion point in the System Editor.

Press	To Move the Insertion Point
↑	Up one line
↓	Down one line
←	Left one character
→	Right one character
PageUp	Previous screen
PageDown	Next screen
Home	Start of line

Editing Text

Press	To Move the Insertion Point
End	End of line
Ctrl-←	Previous word
Ctrl-→	Next word
Ctrl-Home	Top of document
Ctrl-End	Bottom of document

Inserting Text

The vertical line cursor signifies that you are in Insert mode. In Insert mode, text you type pushes existing text to the right. In Overtype mode, the cursor changes from a vertical line to a block, and text you type replaces text already present. To toggle between Overtype and Insert modes, press the Insert key.

Selecting Text

You can select text with the keyboard or with the mouse. To select a single word with the mouse:

1. Point the mouse at the word you want to select.

2. Double-click mouse button 1.

   To select other units of text:

1. Point the mouse where you want the selection to start.

2. Press and hold button 1.

107

3. Drag the selection to where you want it to end.

4. Release button 1.

   Alternatively, you can:

1. Click mouse button 1 where you want the selection to start.

2. Hold down the Shift key and click mouse button 1 where you want the selection to end.

To select text with the keyboard, press and hold down the Shift key while using the normal cursor movement keys.

Deleting Text

Table 18.2 shows you how to delete text:

Table 18.2 Deleting text in the System Editor.

Press	To Delete
Backspace	Single character to the left
Delete	Single character to the right (no text can be selected)
Delete	Selected text

Undo

You can undo the last edit you performed. Undo reverses the last continuous insertion or deletion you performed. To Undo:

- Press Alt-Backspace.

Editing Text

Saving Your Work

You do not need to name a file to type text. As shown in Figure 18.2, the document is given the default name Untitled until you save it.

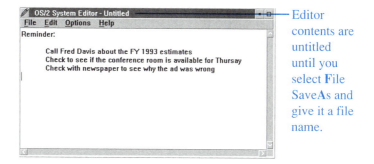

Editor contents are untitled until you select File SaveAs and give it a file name.

Figure 18.2 System Editor with unsaved work called Untitled.

Untitled documents are discarded if you close the editor without saving. To save text:

1. Select File Save As or File Save.

2. Select the disk and directory, and type a new file name.

3. Select a file type (text, OS/2 command, or DOS command).

4. Press Enter.

Using the Clipboard

You can use the Clipboard throughout OS/2 to move and copy text from one place to another. To use the Clipboard,

Lesson 18

you select the text you want to move or copy, copy or cut it to the Clipboard, and then paste the text into a new location. To *copy* text to the Clipboard:

1. Select the text you want to copy.

2. Press Ctrl-Insert.

What's the Clipboard? The *Clipboard* is an area of memory used to temporarily store data you want to move or copy. You put data into the Clipboard using the Cut or Copy commands. When you cut data to the Clipboard, you are moving it from its original location to the Clipboard. This is also called *deleting to the Clipboard*. When you copy data to the Clipboard, the original data remains intact. You use the Paste command to copy data from the Clipboard into a program. Copy and Paste work in all OS/2, WIN-OS/2, and DOS windows. Cut works only in PM and Windows programs. You can use the Clipboard to copy or move data within the same program, or between different programs.

To *cut* text to the Clipboard (similar to copy, but text is deleted in its original location):

1. Select the text you want to copy.

2. Press Shift-Delete.

To paste text from the Clipboard into a new location:

1. Move the insertion point to the new location.

2. Press Shift-Insert.

110

Editing Text

To replace a section of text with the contents of the Clipboard:

1. Select the section you want to replace.

2. Press Shift-Insert.

Enhanced File Editor

You *can* use the Enhanced File Editor like you use the OS/2 System Editor. However, you should not use it to edit OS/2 system files. Most of the basic keystrokes and techniques are the same. The Enhanced File Editor offers enhancements including formatting, printing, and macros. See the on-line documentation for more on how to use the Enhanced File Editor.

Don't Use the Enhanced File Editor to Edit System Files! When the Enhanced File Editor wraps lines of text, it inserts line breaks—which can ruin CONFIG.SYS and other system files. Use the System Editor instead.

In this lesson, you learned how to edit text in OS/2. In the next lesson, you'll learn about the Time Management applications.

Lesson 19
Managing Time with the Planning Applets

In this lesson, you'll learn how to use OS/2's planning applications for time and information management.

Managing Time

You can use the Calendar and Daily Planner applets for scheduling and planning, as well as maintaining a database of past activities. They also include an alarm clock and a telephone dialer.

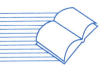

And a Piglet Is a Small Pig An *applet* is a small applications program—like the Calendar, Spreadsheet, or Dialer that come with OS/2 2.0.

Integrating the Planning Applets

The key to making the planning applets work together is to assign the same PM Diary Planner file to each applet. You do this by specifying the same file name in the master planner setting for Alarms (within Alarms), and in the parameters field for each of the following applets:

- Alarms
- Calendar
- Activities List
- Monthly Planner
- Daily Planner

Day by Day The PM Diary Planner file is used to store your appointments, dates, and events. To coordinate your planning applets, they all should use the same PM Diary Planner file. The *master planner file* is the file—that is, the PM Diary Planner file—in which the Alarm applet stores alarms you set. Ideally, all applets should use the same master planner file.

To set the master planner file for Alarms, follow these steps:

1. Open Alarms.
2. Select Customize.
3. Select Set master planner file.
4. Select the appropriate file from the list shown (note the name and location for later use).
5. Press Enter.

If you have never saved a planning entry in the daily planner, a PM Diary Planner file does not yet exist. These files have the extension .D. To create a PM Diary Planner file:

Lesson 19

1. Double-click on the Daily Planner icon in the Productivity folder.

2. Type anything at all into the Description of Activity field—it does not have to be a real activity (for example, just type A and then press the Backspace key to delete the A).

3. Select File Save.

4. Type a file name in the Save As Filename box (for example, type `MyPlan`)—do not type the .D extension.

5. Select Save.

6. Close the Daily Planner applet and follow the procedure to set the master planner file in the Alarms applet.

To specify the same master planner file for use in Calendar, Activities List, Daily Planner, and Monthly Planner:

1. Open the Productivity folder.

2. Click mouse button 2 on the Calendar object icon (and later on the other three applet object icons).

3. Click on the arrow to the right of the word **O**pen.

4. Click on Settings to display the notebook shown in Figure 19.1.

5. Click in the Working directory box, and type the location you used when setting the master planning file for Alarms.

6. Click in the Parameters box, and type the name of the PM Diary Planner file noted above.

7. Double-click on the Title Bar icon to close the Settings notebook.

Repeat these steps for each of the four applets.

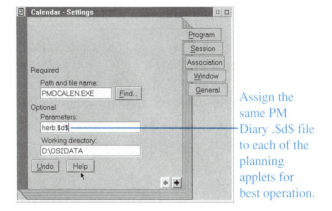

Figure 19.1 Setting the planning applets to use the same .D (PM Diary Planner) file.

Alarms

To open Alarms from the Productivity folder, double-click on the Alarms object icon. The window shown in Figure 19.2 is displayed.

Setting Alarms

To set an alarm:

1. Select Set Alarm from the Alarms menu or press Ctrl-A to display the Set Alarm window, shown in Figure 19.3.

Lesson 19

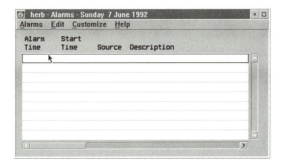

Figure 19.2 The Alarm object's main screen.

2. Click on the day, hour, and minute adjustment arrows to select the day and time (or just type the information).

3. Select a graphic, if desired, for display in the Alarm pop-up window.

4. Type a comment, if desired, for display in the Alarm pop-up window.

5. Select a tune to use as the alarm's sound.

6. Select Activate first Alarm time occurrence only for a one-time alarm, or Activate every Alarm time occurrence for a repeating alarm.

7. To create an audible alarm only, deselect PopUp.

Monthly Planner

Use the Monthly Planner to review a whole month's scheduled events (alarms) at a glance. You can also use it for quick access to the Daily Planner in point-and-shoot fashion. Double-click on the date you want to plan, and it automatically opens the Daily Planner for that date.

Managing Time with the Planning Applets

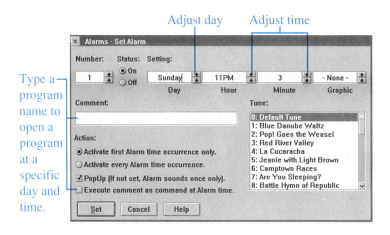

Figure 19.3 The Set Alarm window.

Daily Planner

You can use the Daily Planner to enter and view daily activities. You can use it as a scheduler, as a way to keep track of time spent, or both. Daily entries are created as shown in Figure 19.4.

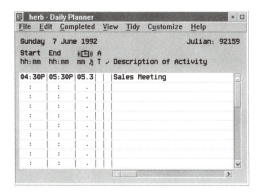

Figure 19.4 Using the Daily Planner as a scheduler.

117

Lesson 19

Planner Archive

The Planner Archive lets you view all archived activities from an archive file ($DA). Archive files are created from the Daily Planner.

Calendar

You can use the Calendar both as a calendar and as an element in the planning applets.

Why Are the View Options Unavailable? You cannot use the Calendar View options until you have opened a Daily Planner file. Until you create and save a Daily Planner file, no files are listed in the File Open window for Calendar. You create a Daily Planner file by making and saving a planning entry using the Daily Planner. Once you've done that, you can use the calendar as a reference, as well as for making entries into the Daily Planner file.

Activities List

You use the Activities List to show all current Daily Planner activities. You can print, view, and sort the Activities List. To sort the list, select View Sort from the menu and select the appropriate criteria.

Tune Editor

Use the Tune Editor to create and edit short tunes for use with the Alarms object.

To Do List

You can use the To Do List to make reminder notes of chores.

To Do List Archive

Use the To Do List archive to view, sort, and print lists of completed items from the To Do List.

Database

The Database applet is a convenient repository for addresses and telephone numbers. You can also use it to dial your phone.

In this lesson, you learned about the time and planning utilities. Next, you'll get a quick look at each of OS/2's other productivity tools.

Lesson 20
Touring the Productivity Applets

In this lesson, you'll learn a little about each of OS/2's remaining productivity utilities and applications.

Spreadsheet

The Spreadsheet applet provides basic spreadsheet capabilities for working with simple sets of calculations. It does not provide graphics, macros, or other advanced features. If you require those features, you should use a dedicated spreadsheet application program.

PM Chart

PM Chart, by Micrografx, is the most sophisticated of OS/2's applications and utilities. You use PM Chart to create drawings, graphs, charts, and symbols.

Symbolism A *symbol* is a completed component of any drawing—PM Chart lets you save a collection of symbols as a clip-art library.

120

Sticky Pad

You use the Sticky Pad to place reminder notes in windows. To create a sticky pad sheet:

1. Open and size the window into which you want a reminder to be placed.

2. Open the Sticky Pad applet.

3. Drag a sticky pad sheet into the window where it's wanted.

4. Type the text of the note.

5. Click mouse button 1 on the sticky pad sheet's Minimize button.

You can create up to 10 sticky pad sheets, as shown in Figure 20.1. To expand a sticky pad sheet so you can read its text, double-click button 1 on the number corresponding to the page you want. You can attach different sheets to different windows, or all to the same window. However, the Sticky Pad applet must remain open to access the sheets.

Picture Viewer

You can use the Picture Viewer to display and print metafiles (.MET) and picture interchange format files (.PIF). You can use it to display a spool file (.SPL) that contains an OS/2 format picture. You can also use the Picture Viewer to transfer pictures to and from the Clipboard. Once displayed in the Picture Viewer, you can save pictures in .MET or .PIF format.

Lesson 20

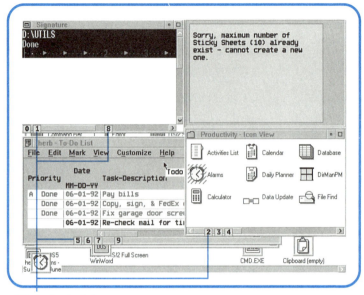

Minimized sticky note pages

Figure 20.1 Making window-specific reminders with Sticky Pad.

PM Terminal

PM Terminal is a terminal emulation program (also known as a communications program). You can use Terminal to communicate and transfer data, usually by modem or via direct COM port connection, between two computers.

It's Not What You Think PM Terminal's terminology is somewhat different from that used by other communications programs. This makes setup potentially confusing. You set up Terminal by selecting options among profiles. A *profile* is a (usually) user-defined set of options. Most user problems result from improperly predefined profile options.

System

Five additional applets are provided for monitoring, facilitating, and enhancing system use and performance. Two of these, Data Update and Clipboard, are virtually automatic and are used by the system as necessary.

Pulse

Pulse displays your computer's activity over a 150-second period. When you open Pulse from the Productivity folder, it displays a graphic like that shown in Figure 20.2. The graph shows the percentage of the CPU (central processing unit) used.

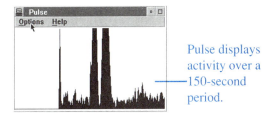

Pulse displays activity over a 150-second period.

Figure 20.2   Using Pulse to measure CPU activity.

Icon Editor

You can edit OS/2 icons with the Icon Editor. You can open the Icon Editor directly by double-clicking on its icon in the Productivity folder. Alternatively, you can open the Icon Editor by clicking on the Edit button in the General section of the Settings notebook for any object.

Seek and Scan Files (PM Seek)

You can use Seek and Scan Files to search for files by name and/or by text. To use Seek and Scan Files from the productivity folder, double-click on the Seek and Scan icon.

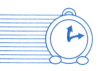

Quicker Seeking You can start Seek and Scan Files from the OS/2 command line by typing `PMSEEK file text` and pressing Enter. For example, `PMSEEK *.DOC dog` searches for all .DOC files on the current drive that contain the string `dog`.

Clipboard

You use the Clipboard to exchange data among applications; it happens automatically—you don't have to open the Clipboard. Review Lesson 18 for more on how to use the Clipboard for copying and pasting. You can open the Clipboard directly to change its status (from public to private or vice versa—see Lesson 22), to make a single transfer of data, or to change the way a data item is displayed.

In Lessons 18 through 20, you learned about OS/2's productivity tools. For users who need DOS, Lessons 21 and 22 will get you started.

Lesson 21
Running DOS in OS/2

In this lesson, you will learn how to use the OS/2 DOS command line.

Emulating DOS 5

OS/2 emulates DOS 5 in *virtual DOS machines*, or *VDM*s. With few exceptions, a full-screen VDM acts just like DOS 5 running on an 8086 computer. Moreover, OS/2 provides the advantages of multitasking, HPFS disk performance, and the ability to configure DOS settings without rebooting.

Virtual What?   When OS/2 runs a DOS session, it carves out a work area that emulates the behavior of an 8086 computer (only much faster). Each DOS session gets its own "virtual" 8086 workspace, sometimes called a *virtual DOS machine* (VDM)— a section of RAM that looks and acts like DOS 5 running on an 8086 computer.

125

Lesson 21

Limitations of OS/2's DOS

Most DOS applications work just as well, if not better, in a VDM than in real DOS. Some, however, don't work well or don't work at all. For the most part, the OS/2 VDM doesn't work with DOS programs that:

- Directly manipulate the hardware, especially the disk.

- Require exclusive access to the 80386 control registers.

- Are very timing-sensitive (as are, for example, some games and fax cards).

See the README file that comes with OS/2 2.0 for a complete list of applications, problems, and solutions. To view the README file, open the Information folder and double-click on README.

Opening a DOS Command Line Session

To open a DOS command line session:

1. Open the OS/2 System folder.

2. Open the Command Prompts folder.

3. Double-click the kind of DOS session you want (full-screen or windowed).

Running DOS in OS/2

Closing a DOS Command Line Session

You can close an OS/2 DOS full-screen session in two ways:

- Type EXIT from the command line.

  or

- Select Close from the Window list.

You can close a windowed DOS session in the same two ways, plus two more:

- Double-click on the DOS Title Bar icon.

  or

- Open the DOS object menu (click button 2 on the Title Bar icon) and select the Close option.

If the DOS application you're running works in an OS/2 window (a few graphics-based programs cannot run in a window), you can press Alt-Home at any time to toggle between full-screen and windowed views. Once in a window, you can additionally use the windowed closing methods.

Working at the DOS Command Line

You work at the DOS command line the way you usually do in real DOS. Run programs and utilities as you normally do.

Almost all programs, directory, and filing commands work just as they would under real DOS.

Using AUTOEXEC.BAT

OS/2 puts a special AUTOEXEC.BAT on your root directory. You can change it to meet your needs. There is no dedicated CONFIG.SYS for a VDM. Some DOS-specific commands are contained in the OS/2 CONFIG.SYS file. For the most part, however, you control DOS settings from the DOS object's Session DOS Settings menu.

Configure and Customize DOS uses two files to configure and customize the DOS operating system: CONFIG.SYS and AUTOEXEC.BAT. CONFIG.SYS contains configuration and memory settings. AUTOEXEC.BAT processes commands to customize a particular setup. OS/2 2.0 provides AUTOEXEC.BAT for customizing DOS setup. Session configuration is controlled using the DOS Settings button in the Session tab in the DOS Settings Notebook. The CONFIG.SYS file on your OS/2 root directory is for all of OS/2—not for a particular DOS session.

Using the Clipboard in a DOS Session

One of the chief benefits of working in a windowed DOS session is the ability to copy and paste among DOS, Windows, and OS/2 windows. To do this, you use the Clipboard.

To copy text from a DOS window to the Clipboard using the keyboard:

1. Press and release the Alt key.

2. Press K (for Mark).

3. Use the cursor keys to move the cursor to where you want the selection to start.

4. Use Shift-←, Shift-→, Shift-↑, and Shift-↓ to select the area you want to copy (see Figure 21.1).

5. Press Alt, Y (Copy) to copy the marked text to the Clipboard.

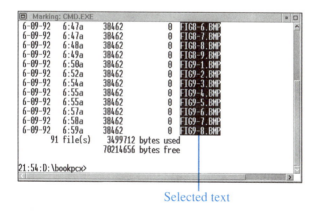

Selected text

Figure 21.1 Selecting text in a DOS command window.

Quicker Copying Once you've selected text in a DOS or OS/2 window, simply press Enter to copy the selection to the Clipboard.

Lesson 21

To paste the contents of the Clipboard into most OS/2 Presentation Manager applications:

1. Switch to the application where you want to paste.

2. Press Shift-Insert to paste.

To paste the Clipboard into a DOS window:

- Press Alt, P.

Stop Those Returns When pasting data into a DOS window, you often don't want the data to include a carriage return. To suppress the final carriage return, hold down the Shift key while you paste. You cannot suppress the carriage return when pasting data from a DOS window into an OS/2 Presentation Manager window.

Using the Clipboard with a Mouse

To copy text into the Clipboard using the mouse:

1. Click on the DOS Title Bar icon.

2. Click on Mark.

3. Select text by dragging mouse button 1 across the selection.

4. Click on the DOS Title Bar icon.

5. Click on Copy.

Running DOS in OS/2

To paste into a DOS window using the mouse:

1. Click on the DOS Title Bar icon.

2. Click on Paste (hold down the Shift key to suppress a final carriage return).

Clipboard Doesn't Work! If you are using a private Clipboard in a WIN-OS/2 session, you will not be able to paste data from a DOS or OS/2 session into the Windows application. You must first use the Options menu command in the Clipboard to make the Clipboard public. Alternatively, you can use the File Export and Import commands to transfer the current contents between an OS/2 or DOS window and WIN-OS/2 (WIN-OS/2 is OS/2's emulation of Microsoft Windows). For more on public versus private status for the Clipboard, see Lesson 22.

In this lesson, you learned how to use OS/2's virtual DOS machine to emulate DOS 5. In the next lesson, you will learn how to run Windows programs under OS/2.

131

Lesson 22
Running WIN-OS/2

In this lesson, you will learn a number of ways to run Windows programs under OS/2, and the differences among the approaches.

Running Windows

OS/2 lets users run Windows programs using WIN-OS/2. WIN-OS/2 is based on Windows 3.0. For the most part, you can use WIN-OS/2 exactly as you use Windows. When you start a WIN-OS/2 session, the WIN-OS/2 Program Manager looks identical to Program Manager as run from Windows.

You can run most Windows programs unmodified in WIN-OS/2, exactly as you run them under Windows 3. You can install most Windows programs into the Program Manager or into any of the various program groups, just as you can under Windows 3. There are a few exceptions—users who encounter problems should see the README file that comes with OS/2 for a list of applications and special considerations.

If you are unfamiliar with Windows or you would like a more detailed guide to using Microsoft Windows, I suggest the following books by Sams:

The First Book of Windows 3.1, Bestseller Edition, by Jack Nimersheim

10 Minute Guide to Windows 3.1 by Kate Barnes

Opening WIN-OS/2

OS/2 offers three ways to open Windows programs:

1. Open WIN-OS/2 from the Command Prompts folder, which is in the OS/2 System folder. Run the application from the WIN-OS/2 Program Manager using normal Windows procedures.

2. Create a program object for the Windows application, and open it from a folder (see Lesson 12).

3. Run a Windows application directly from the OS/2 command line (just type its name—for example, type `AMIPRO`).

Regardless of the method you use, OS/2 loads a copy of WIN-OS/2 before running the program. Most Windows programs act similarly under WIN-OS/2 and Windows. The only differences you will encounter are the ways Windows programs interact with the operating environment:

- The Clipboard can be private or public.

- WIN-OS/2's Program Manager cannot run non-Windows applications.

133

- WIN-OS/2 can't run programs that require Enhanced Mode.

Private or Public? When you make the Clipboard *private*, OS/2 creates a separate (local) Clipboard for each distinct WIN-OS/2 session. OS/2 creates an overall Clipboard for OS/2 and DOS windows. Windows programs running in the same WIN-OS/2 session can exchange data with each other, but not with applications running outside that WIN-OS/2 session. When you make the Clipboard *public*, all applications share a single Clipboard and can exchange data with each other.

Windows 3.1 and Enhanced Mode When you try to run some Windows applications, you may get a message like This program requires Windows Enhanced Mode or This program requires a later version of Windows. As this book goes to press, OS/2 does not yet support Enhanced Mode or programs that require Windows 3.1. IBM will be adding Windows 3.1 features and support shortly—perhaps by the time you're reading this book. Very few programs require Enhanced Mode. Most that do require Enhanced Mode are being rewritten to run directly under OS/2.

A second difference between WIN-OS/2 and Windows is that WIN-OS/2 itself can't run non-WIN-OS/2 DOS programs. However, since OS/2 can run DOS programs, you usually won't be giving up any capabilities. You'll just be taking a slightly different route.

Closing WIN-OS/2

How you close a WIN-OS/2 session depends on how you open it. If you open a program from the Program Manager:

1. Close the application using its own Close or Exit command.

2. Close the Program Manager.

To close a Windows program you open from the OS/2 Desktop or from the OS/2 command line:

- Close the application using its own Close or Exit command.

In the latter case, OS/2 automatically closes the underlying WIN-OS/2 support.

Setting the Display Method

OS/2 offers two display methods for Windows application programs:

- Full screen

- Windowed (also called "seamless")

Full-screen WIN-OS/2 looks identical to actual Windows running in standard mode. If you don't need to run Windows, OS/2, and DOS programs on-screen at the same time, full-screen WIN-OS/2 provides slightly faster performance than does windowed.

Under the windowed or seamless approach, OS/2 runs WIN-OS/2 in an OS/2 window on the Desktop. You can

Lesson 22

size, move, minimize, maximize, cut, copy, and paste, just as you can with ordinary OS/2 applications.

To set a Windows application to full-screen or windowed:

1. Click mouse button 2 on a closed Windows program icon.

2. Click on the arrow to the right of **Open**.

3. Click on Settings.

4. Click on Session.

5. Select WIN-OS/2 full screen or WIN-OS/2 window.

6. Double-click on the Title Bar icon to close the settings.

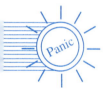

Can't Make WIN-OS/2 Seamless If you apply the procedure shown to a WIN-OS/2 object, you'll discover that WIN-OS/2 is a DOS program—not a Windows program. To create a seamless WIN-OS/2 session that itself can launch multiple Windows programs, create a program object that runs PROGMAN.EXE (the Program Manager, on \OS2\MDOS\WINOS2\). Then proceed as above to set the session to full-screen or windowed.

Running Alone versus Sharing WIN-OS/2

You have yet another choice when running Windows applications in WIN-OS/2. You can dedicate one WIN-OS/2 session per application, or you can run several applications within the same WIN-OS/2 session. The trade-off is memory usage versus protection. Using a dedicated WIN-OS/2 for each program uses more memory, but the extra isolation virtually eliminates UAEs and GPFs.

UAEs and GPFs   Under Windows 3.0, if a program accesses memory outside its own virtual space, it causes an *Unrecoverable Application Error* (*UAE*) or a *General Protection Fault* (*GPF*). UAEs almost always require rebooting when using Windows under DOS.

In this lesson, you learned the basics of running WIN-OS/2. In the next lesson, you'll learn how to work in WIN-OS/2.

Lesson 23

Using and Managing WIN-OS/2

This lesson tells how to close, configure, and set up Windows programs to run under OS/2. It also discusses the use of the Clipboard and printing using ATM (Adobe Type Manager).

Configuring a WIN-OS/2 Session

Use WIN-OS/2's Control Panel and Setup applications to change and configure the Windows environment as you would in Windows. Be sure to check the Save box when closing WIN-OS/2. The settings stored in WIN.INI and SYSTEM.INI on \OS2\MDOS\WINOS2 are used by all Windows applications. You do not need to make changes individually for each Windows program you use.

Changes Don't Take When you make a change using Windows controls, the change affects only that session and sessions started thereafter. If you have independent WIN-OS/2 sessions active at the same time, they will not be affected until closed and restarted. Beware, however, of making distinct changes in independent sessions. Only the last one changed will "take."

Using and Managing WIN-OS/2

Adding a Windows Application to a Folder

You can add Windows applications to any WIN-OS/2 program group, to the Desktop folder, or to any other folder. To add Windows applications to a program group, follow the procedures in your Windows manual. To add a Windows application to an OS/2 Desktop folder:

1. Open the Templates folder.

2. Open the target folder.

3. Drag a program object from the Templates folder and drop it in the target folder.

4. Click on Create; this brings up the Program Settings menu.

5. Type the path and name for the application.

6. Type any parameters needed.

7. Type the working directory (only if different from the application's location).

8. Click on the Session tab.

9. Click on WIN-OS/2 window or full screen.

10. Select or deselect Separate Session, as needed.

11. Double-click on the Title Bar icon to close.

Using the Clipboard in WIN-OS/2

In OS/2, the Clipboard can be *public* or *private*. In private mode, you can use the Clipboard only to transfer data among applications within that specific WIN-OS/2 session. When the Clipboard is public, you can transfer data among Windows, OS/2 and windowed DOS sessions. To change the status of the Clipboard:

1. Open the Clipboard; restore it if it's already open.

2. Click on Options.

3. If a check mark appears by Public, the Clipboard is public; remove the check mark to make the Clipboard private.

Printing in WIN-OS/2

Printing in WIN-OS/2 is identical to printing in Windows. Most Windows programs list a **P**rint command from a **F**ile menu. Select File Print and follow the application's own printing instructions.

Using the Adobe Type Manager

OS/2 provides the Adobe Type Manager 2.0 for use in WIN-OS/2. ATM 2.0 provides scalable typefaces for display and printing for Windows applications. To use the Adobe Type Manager:

1. Open WIN-OS/2.

Using and Managing WIN-OS/2

2. Double-click on the ATM Control Panel icon; this reveals the window shown in Figure 23.1.

3. Click the On box.

4. Click on the Exit button to close the ATM Control Panel.

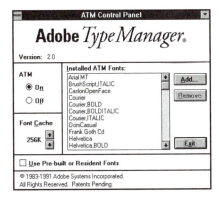

Figure 23.1 The Adobe Type Manager control panel.

Application Doesn't Print Correctly While ATM generally provides excellent typeface support, it can interfere with the operation of some programs. TurboTax for Windows, for example, sometimes does not print properly with the HP LaserJet printers when ATM is active. If you experience printing problems using programs that provide their own special font support, try turning ATM off before printing from that application.

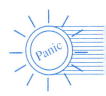

141

Lesson 23

Adding ATM fonts

Under some circumstances, ATM fonts fail to install during OS/2 installation. A symptom that this has occurred is that the ATM icon appears crossed out when WIN-OS/2 is loading. If the ATM icon is crossed out, and if ATM is turned on, OS/2 did not install the fonts. To install the ATM fonts:

1. Open the ATM Control Panel from WIN-OS/2's Program Manager.

2. Verify that ATM is turned on.

3. Click on Add.

4. Insert the last OS/2 Printer Driver diskette into drive A.

5. Select A: as the source drive from the Add fonts menu.

6. When a list of fonts appears, select all on the list.

7. Click on Add.

In this lesson, you learned how to configure and set up Windows programs to run under OS/2. Congratulations! You've completed the *10 Minute Guide to OS/2 2.0*. Ready for a little post-graduate work and review? In the last part of this book, you'll find supplemental information on OS/2's daunting installation procedures, a summary of common OS/2 procedures, and a reference illuminating the most common OS/2 commands.

Overtime

Up and Running with OS/2

Using DISKCOPY to Make Backups of Program Disks

Before you install any program on your hard disk or run it from your floppy drive, make *backup copies* of the original program disks to avoid damaging the original disks. (Although you don't have to format the blank disks before you begin, the disks must match the program disks in number, size, and density.)

Protect the Disks Before using DISKCOPY, write-protect the original disks. For 3.5-inch disks, slide the write-protect tab so you can see through the window. For 5.25-inch disks, apply a write-protect sticker over the write-protect notch.

1. Change to the drive and directory that contains the DOS DISKCOPY file. For example, if the file is in the C:\DOS directory, type `cd\dos` at the C:> prompt, and press Enter.

2. Type `diskcopy a: a:` or `diskcopy b: b:`, depending on which drive you're using to make the copies, and press Enter.

3. Insert the original program disk you want to copy into the specified drive and press Enter.

4. Follow the on-screen messages to complete the process.

5. Remove the disk from the drive and label it to match the name of the original program disk.

6. Repeat the process until you have copies of all the program disks.

Backing Up Your System Before Installing OS/2

Before you install OS/2, it's a good idea to back up files that you have stored on your PC's hard drive. If you're installing OS/2 for the first time, you might want to format your hard drive during installation to install the High Performance File System (HPFS). Remember, everything is erased during formatting.

If you use the BACKUP command, it's a good idea to prepare your diskettes in advance, labeling them with the date and disk number. If your disks have been numbered consecutively, it will be possible for you to feed them back to your PC in order during the RESTORE.

You can decide if you want to back up all of your fixed drive or just parts of it. A complete system backup is a good idea if you want to remove OS/2 and put your previous system back in place.

- To back up drive C, type BACKUP C:*.* A: /S on a DOS or OS/2 command line.

- If you want to back up only selected applications and all of their files, for instance all of your word processing subdirectory, go to the application and type `BACKUP C: A:`.

If you decide to back up just your applications and data files, you can also use the XCOPY command instead of BACKUP. XCOPY duplicates on floppy disks the file structure you see on the original disk. To use XCOPY:

- Go to the selected subdirectory and then type `XCOPY C:\ A:\ /S`.

Different Types of Installation

OS/2 can be installed in three different ways:

- OS/2 only (described on the inside front cover)
- Dual Boot
- Boot Manager

OS/2 only

Use the OS/2 only installation if you are sure that you will not need to access real DOS on your computer. If you select the HPFS (High Performance File System) option, you can install DOS only by reformatting your hard disk. The OS/2-only installation provides near-perfect emulation of an 8086 computer running DOS 5.0, and similar emulation of Windows running in Standard mode. To access Windows Enhanced 386 mode or the protected-mode features of an 80286 or 80386 from DOS, you will need to install either Dual Boot or Boot Manager.

Dual Boot

A Dual Boot installation is the easiest way to continue to use real DOS while installing OS/2 2.0. If you have ample disk space on your boot drive (drive C), Dual Boot is the easiest way to move to OS/2 while keeping full DOS capabilities. Dual Boot does not require formatting your hard drive. Further, Dual Boot doesn't let you take advantage of HPFS on your OS/2 boot partition. You can format other partitions as HPFS, but the boot partition must be formatted as FAT (File Allocation Table) for Dual Boot.

Boot Manager

If you need access to real DOS, Boot Manager is the most powerful option, as well as the most difficult to set up. To use Boot Manager, you must reformat all or part of your hard drive. Once done, Boot Manager lets you install multiple operating systems on the same computer—DOS, OS/2 1.0, OS/2 2.0, AIX, and others.

What's Best for You?

Consider your needs as well as how much reformatting you are willing to do when you choose a type of installation.

Unfortunately, what's best isn't always what's easiest. If you have a brand-new system with no operating system at all, your best choices are OS/2 only or Boot Manager—depending on whether or not you will need access to real DOS. OS/2 only is undoubtedly easier, but may not be an option if you really do need real DOS.

If you have a new system with neither DOS nor OS/2 installed, avoid the Dual Boot installation, as it sometimes creates problems. The isolation provided by Boot Manager is well worth the extra installation difficulty.

If you have an existing system with DOS installed, and you want to move slowly to OS/2 while keeping as much of your current setup as possible, a Dual Boot system is the easiest route. You will have to exercise caution when using commands such as CHKDSK from DOS, however, because the DOS version of some commands does not recognize certain OS/2 features (such as extended attributes). However, Dual Boot does offer the quickest and least traumatic way to move to OS/2 for an existing DOS system.

Speed

For disks and partitions that will be accessed only by OS/2, you have two options: FAT and HPFS. FAT (the same system that's used by DOS) is more subject to fragmentation and is somewhat slower than HPFS. However, FAT drives can be read and written by real DOS. If you select a Dual Boot or a Boot Manager installation, then at least part of your system must be formatted as FAT.

If you are installing an OS/2-only system, and if you have 6M or more of main memory (RAM), you should consider HPFS for the speed and reliability benefits.

How much faster is HPFS? Depending on the file and disk size, file operations are from five to ten times faster under HPFS than the same operations using FAT. For most users, HPFS is a great way to speed up all programs running under OS/2—including DOS and Windows programs.

Running Multiple Operating Systems

If you want to run multiple operating systems, the Boot Manager is the only choice. Furthermore, if you have a two-SCSI disk system on which you want to retain access to DOS, the Boot Manager also is usually required because of the way SCSI device drivers are written.

To install OS/2 Dual Boot or Boot Manager, use the OS/2 Installation guide packaged with OS/2. IBM even has an 800 number to call if you have problems: (800) 237-5511.

Uninstalling OS/2

Under some circumstances, you may need to remove OS/2 from a system on which it was installed. Use the following procedures to remove OS/2.

Removing OS/2 from an OS/2-Only System

To remove OS/2 from your PC:

1. Boot DOS with a disk that contains FDISK.
2. Type FDISK on the command line.
3. Select the OS/2 partition.
4. Press Enter to display the Options pull-down menu.
5. Choose Delete partition.

Removing OS/2 Files from a Dual Boot System

Use the Dual Boot object to boot real DOS. At the C prompt, type:

```
ATTRIB -S -H -R OS2KRNL
DEL OS2KRNL
ATTRIB -S -H -R OS2BOOT
DEL OS2BOOT
ATTRIB -S -H -R OS2LDR
DEL OS2LDR.*
ATTRIB -S -H -R EA*.*
DEL EA*.* /P
```

Type y to confirm the deletion of EADATA; type n for any other files matching EA*.*. Next, type

```
ATTRIB -S -H -R WP*.*
DEL WP*.* /P
```

Type y to confirm the deletion of WPROOT; type n for any other files matching WP*.*.

Using any method you choose, delete all files and subdirectories and then remove the following directories:

- C:\DESKTOP
- C:\OS2
- C:\DELETE
- C:\NOWHERE
- C:\SPOOL
- C:\PSFONTS

The Easy Way Out You can use the tried-and-true DEL *.* followed by RD approach, but that's very time-consuming and error prone. Instead, if it is available, use DOSSHELL, the Windows 3.1 File Manager, Xtree, or some other DOS shell that simplifies file and directory deletion.

Removing Boot Manager and HPFS Partitions

1. Open an OS/2 Command Prompt window.

2. Type FDISK.

3. Make the disk containing the new single permanent operating system Startable (usually DOS or OS/2 1.0).

4. Select Delete Partition for all OS/2 partitions you want to remove.

5. Select Delete Partition for the Boot Manager Partition.

6. Create new partitions from the newly deleted partitions, as desired.

7. Select Save and then Exit.

8. Reboot your system. OS/2 is now gone. See your alternative operating system manual for how to reformat the deleted partitions.

Look Out! Be very careful when removing files and directories. Some Windows programs install drivers and dynamic link libraries on the WIN-OS/2 subdirectory.

Removing OS/2 Files from a Dual Boot System

Use the Dual Boot object to boot real DOS. At the C prompt, type:

```
ATTRIB -S -H -R OS2KRNL
DEL OS2KRNL
ATTRIB -S -H -R OS2BOOT
DEL OS2BOOT
ATTRIB -S -H -R OS2LDR
DEL OS2LDR.*
ATTRIB -S -H -R EA*.*
DEL EA*.* /P
```

Type Y to confirm the deletion of EADATA; type N for any other files matching EA*.*. Next, type

```
ATTRIB -S -H -R WP*.*
DEL WP*.* /P
```

Type Y to confirm the deletion of WPROOT; type N for any other files matching WP*.*.

Using any method you choose, delete all files and subdirectories and then remove the following directories:

- C:\DESKTOP
- C:\OS2
- C:\DELETE
- C:\NOWHERE
- C:\SPOOL
- C:\PSFONTS

The Easy Way Out You can use the tried-and-true DEL *.* followed by RD approach, but that's very time-consuming and error prone. Instead, if it is available, use DOSSHELL, the Windows 3.1 File Manager, Xtree, or some other DOS shell that simplifies file and directory deletion.

Removing Boot Manager and HPFS Partitions

1. Open an OS/2 Command Prompt window.

2. Type FDISK.

3. Make the disk containing the new single permanent operating system Startable (usually DOS or OS/2 1.0).

4. Select Delete Partition for all OS/2 partitions you want to remove.

5. Select Delete Partition for the Boot Manager Partition.

6. Create new partitions from the newly deleted partitions, as desired.

7. Select Save and then Exit.

8. Reboot your system. OS/2 is now gone. See your alternative operating system manual for how to reformat the deleted partitions.

Look Out! Be very careful when removing files and directories. Some Windows programs install drivers and dynamic link libraries on the WIN-OS/2 subdirectory.

Summary of Common OS/2 Procedures

This section is a summary of common OS/2 procedures. For more complete information, see the appropriate lesson as indicated in the text.

Opening, Closing, Resizing, and Moving Windows (Lessons 3 and 4)

To open an object window follow these steps:

1. Open the folder that contains the object.

2. Select the object by clicking on it or using the cursor keys.

3. Double-click on the object, press Enter, or select the Open command from the object pop-up menu.

   To close an object window:

1. Click on the object to give it the focus.

2. Press Alt-F4, double-click the Title Bar icon, or select the Close command from the object pop-up menu.

10 Minute Guide to OS/2 2.0

To drag an object:

1. Point the mouse at the object.

2. Hold down mouse button 2.

3. Move the mouse while holding mouse button 2 to drag the object to a new location. Release the mouse button when the object is where you want it.

To resize an object window:

1. Move the mouse pointer on a window border until it assumes the shape of a double-headed arrow.

2. Press and hold either mouse button.

3. Drag the border until the window is the size you want.

4. Release the mouse button.

To move a window:

1. Point the mouse at the title bar.

2. Press and hold either mouse button.

3. Drag the window to a new position.

4. Release the mouse button.

To maximize a window:

- Press Alt-F10 or click the Maximize button.

To minimize a window:

- Press Alt-F9 or click the Minimize button.

Summary of Common OS/2 Procedures

To restore a window:

- Press Alt-F5 or double-click on the title bar.

Navigating OS/2 (Lessons 3 and 4)

To see a list of open windows and to switch to any window:

1. Press Ctrl-Esc for the Window list.

2. Double-click on the title of the window you want.

   To open the Window list with the mouse:

- Click mouse buttons 1 and 2 together on a blank area on the desktop.

   To select an object in a folder with the keyboard:

- Press the first letter of the object's name; if there is more than one matching object, press the letter until the one you want is selected.

   To switch to a visible window with the mouse:

- Click mouse button 1 on any part of the window.

   To rotate among all open tasks—windowed and full-screen, OS/2, WIN-OS/2, and DOS:

- Press Alt-Esc.

   To rotate among all open OS/2 windows:

1. Give any OS/2 window the focus.

2. Press Alt-Tab.

To rotate among all open WIN-OS/2 windows within a WIN-OS/2 session:

1. Make the WIN-OS/2 window active.

2. Press Alt-Tab to cycle through all open windows in that WIN-OS/2 session.

   To expand a hidden list:

   - Click on the down arrow to the right of the item that's showing.

   or

   - Press Alt-↓.

   To cancel the current command:

   - Press the Esc key.

   To give the main desktop the focus:

   - Press Alt-Shift-Tab.

   To move to the top left item in the current window (top left):

   - Press Ctrl-Home.

   To move to the bottom right item in the current window (bottom right):

   - Press Ctrl-End.

   To toggle a main menu bar on or off:

   - Press and release the Alt or F10 key.

Summary of Common OS/2 Procedures

To find the Desktop pop-up menu and shut down with a mouse:

1. Click mouse button 2 on a blank area on the main Desktop.

2. Click on Shut down.

To find the Desktop pop-up and shut down with the keyboard:

1. Press Alt-Shift-Tab (to give the Desktop the focus).

2. Press Ctrl-\ (deselects all icons).

3. Press Shift-F10 (to display the object pop-up menu).

4. Select Shut down.

Copying, Shadowing, and Deleting an Object (Lessons 9, 12, and 13)

To copy an object:

1. Open the folder that contains the object.

2. Click mouse button 2 on the object.

3. Select the Copy option.

4. Select a destination.

5. Click on Copy.

To copy an object by dragging:

1. Open the source and destination folders.
2. Press and hold the Ctrl key.
3. Point the mouse at the object and press and hold mouse button 2.
4. Drag the object to the destination folder.
5. Release the mouse button *before* releasing the Ctrl key.

To create a shadow of an object by dragging:

1. Open the source and destination folders.
2. Press and hold the Ctrl and Shift keys at the same time.
3. Point the mouse at the object; press and hold mouse button 2.
4. Drag the object to the destination folder.
5. Release the mouse button *before* releasing the Ctrl and Shift keys.

To delete an object:

1. Click mouse button 2 on the object.
2. Select the Delete option from the object pop-up menu.

To delete objects or files by dragging:

1. Open the folder or drive containing the object or file.
2. Make sure that the Shredder is visible.
3. Click mouse button 1 on the first item you want to delete.

Summary of Common OS/2 Procedures

4. Press and hold the Ctrl key.

5. Click mouse button 1 on each item you want to delete.

6. Point at any selected item.

7. Drag the items to the Shredder using mouse button 2 until a box appears, indicating that the objects are in position.

8. Release mouse button 2.

9. Confirm the deletion if prompted.

Creating and Renaming Objects (Lessons 13 and 16)

To create a folder or a file object:

1. Open the Templates folder and the target folder.

2. Point the mouse at a template for the kind of object you want to create.

3. Press and hold mouse button 2.

4. Drag the template to the target folder.

5. Release the mouse button—this creates a new object with a generic name.

6. Use the rename procedure to assign a more useful name.

   To create a program object:

1. Open the Templates folder and the target folder.

2. Point the mouse at a Program template.

3. Press and hold mouse button 2.

4. Drag the template to the target folder.

5. Release the mouse button.

6. Fill out the program settings information.

7. Double-click on the Settings Title Bar icon when you're done.

To create a new printer object:

1. Open the Templates folder.

2. Point the mouse at a Printer template.

3. Press and hold mouse button 2.

4. Drag the template to the Desktop.

5. Release the mouse button.

6. Type a name for the printer.

7. Select a printer driver—click on the appropriate driver.

8. Select a printer output target.

9. Double-click the Create Printer Title Bar icon to close.

To rename an object:

1. Press and hold Alt while you click mouse button 1 on the object you want to change; this opens an editable text field.

Summary of Common OS/2 Procedures

2. Type a new name into the text field.
3. Click on the object icon to close the text field.

Command Reference

This section covers the most common OS/2 commands (note that some are inherently similar to their DOS counterparts). You can use the on-line command reference for more help and examples.

For each command given here, the purpose and command type (OS/2, DOS, or both) are listed, followed by an example showing the command with sample parameters, along with a brief explanation. Variables where given are italicized. Switches and additional rules or information are included as needed.

BACKUP (OS/2 and DOS)

Backs up files from one disk to another.

BACKUP D:*.* A:, where D: is the source and A: is the target.

The Data Starts Here! The *source* is a disk, file, document or any other "collection" of information from which data is taken or moved. Your source can be any valid file specification, including disk, path, and wild cards.

The Data Stops Here! The *target* is the destination of a copy operation. Your target can be any valid directory specification; usually one level less specific than the source. For instance, the command COPY C:\DATA\MY.DOC D:\NEWDAT copies a file named MY.DOC from a directory on drive C named DATA (the source) to a directory on drive D named NEWDAT (the target). If you include a different file specification, the new file(s) are renamed as they are copied. If you leave out the target, the file is copied to the current directory.

Switches

/L:*filename*   Creates a BACKUP.LOG.

/D:*mm-dd-yy*   Backs up files that have changed since the date *mm-dd-yy*.

/T:*hh:mm:ss*   Backs up files that have changed since the time *hh:mm:ss*.

/M   Backs up only files that have changed since your last backup.

/A   Adds new backup files to an existing backup on the target (rather than overwriting).

/F:*xxx*   Formats the target disk as size (*xxx* sets the number of kilobytes on target disk: 360, 720, 1,200, 1,440, or 2,880) before backing up files.

/S   Backs up subdirectories beneath the current directory.

161

CD or CHDIR (OS/2 and DOS)

Changes or displays the active directories on a disk.

`CD \OS2`, where \OS2 is a subdirectory.

`CD "C:OS!2 2.0 Desktop"`, where an extended HPFS file name containing spaces is surrounded by quotation marks.

COPY (OS/2 and DOS)

Copies files. Also used to rename, merge, or append files as they are copied.

`COPY *.AAA *.BBB`, where all files matching *.AAA (source) are copied to a series of files named *.BBB (target).

Switches

/A Copies files as ASCII text files. Used after the source file, the /A switch causes COPY to stop after the first ^Z (ASCII 26, the EOF marker). Used after the target, it causes COPY to append a ^Z to the end of the target file.

/B Copies files as binary files. Used after the source, the /B switch tells COPY to copy the entire file, including any ^Zs. Used after the target, it tells COPY not to insert an extra ^Z at the end.

/V Verifies all sectors while copying.

Command Reference

/F   Halts copying if the file contains extended attributes and the target does not support them.

/+   Combines and appends files.

,,   Stamps the new file with the current time and date.

Here are some more examples:

COPY *.AAA + *.BBB *.CCC combines each .AAA and .BBB file pair, where the name matches, to create a new file with the same name and the .CCC extension as the first file in the list.

COPY *.AAA + *.BBB ALLFILES.CCC combines all .AAA and .BBB files to create one file called ALLFILES.CCC.

COPY *.DOC /B + ,, stamps all files with the .DOC extension in the current directory with the current time and date.

COPY FILE.SPL /B LPT1 copies a printer-ready file to the printer (a printer-ready file contains control codes; this is equivalent to selecting the printer-specific button when dragging a file to the printer).

COPY FILE.TXT /A LPT1 copies a plain-text file to the printer.

DATE (OS/2 and DOS)

Examines and sets the system date.

DATE *mm-dd-yy*, where *mm-dd-yy* are the month, day, and year.

163

The order of mm-dd-yy depends on your country information and preferences.

DETACH (OS/2 Only)

Use DETACH to multitask from an OS/2 command line (CMD) session.

> DETACH COPY *.* A:, where all files are copied independently to the target drive (A:).

> **Fire One!** DETACH launches an OS/2 program to run in the background. Use DETACH only when the program is self-completing and does not prompt for additional input or output. Contrast DETACH with START: You cannot switch to a detached process; you *can* switch to a process launched with START.

DIR (OS/2 and DOS)

Displays files and directories.

> DIR C:\JOHNDIR /W, where C:\JOHNDIR are the path and subdirectory and /W is a switch.

Switches

/A:y Displays files with matching attributes *y*, where *y* can be A, H, R, or S (for example, DIR /A:H displays all hidden files; see the ATTRIB command).

Command Reference

/B   Omits directory header information.

/F   Displays fully qualified file names (including drive letter, directory name, and file name).

/L   Displays names in lowercase.

/N   Displays FAT drives in the more detailed HPFS format.

/O:[-]s   Sorts directory using s criteria (- means reverse order), where s can be N (name), E (extension), D (date), S (size), or G (directories grouped after file names).

/P   Pauses after each screen.

/R   Displays long file names on FAT drives (assuming EA DATA.SF is present).

/S   Searches subdirectories.

/W   Displays files in a five-column listing.

ERASE or DEL (OS/2 and DOS)

Deletes or erases one or more files and directories.

DEL *.*, where *.* represents all files in the current directory.

Switches

/P   Prompts you to decide whether to delete each file.

165

/N   Suppresses the Are you sure? prompt when deleting all files.

Here are some more examples:

DEL \XYZ deletes all files in the \XYZ directory (leaves subdirectories alone).

DEL *.DOC/P deletes files with the .DOC extension, prompting at each.

DEL *.*/N deletes all files in the current directory, without prompting Are you sure?.

EXIT (OS/2 and DOS)

Closes an OS/2 or DOS command line session, except for a specific DOS version (bootable DOS), and returns to the previous session or to the Desktop. Be sure to end your current programs before you type EXIT.

FORMAT (OS/2 and DOS)

Prepares a disk or diskette for use. Checks the diskette for defects and marks tracks, sectors, file allocation tables, and a directory on the disk. Unlike DOS, the OS/2 FORMAT command cannot prepare a boot or system diskette (use the installation diskettes or consult an OS/2 shareware BBS for single-boot-disk solutions). Remember that FORMAT erases any information that already exists on the disk being formatted.

FORMAT A: /f:1440, where drive A holds the unformatted diskette, and a switch indicates the size of diskette to be formatted.

Command Reference

The Right Spot! Before you format a hard drive, be certain that an OS/2 partition has been established.

Switches

/ONCE Suppresses the Format Another? prompt.

/4 Formats a 360K diskette in a 1.2M drive.

/T:tracks Lets you specify the number of tracks.

/N:sectors Lets you specify the number of sectors.

/F:xxxx Lets you specify the size of the diskette.

/FS:type Changes a disk's file system (type can be HPFS or FAT). This switch works on hard disks only.

/L Formats an unformatted IBM optical disk.

/V:label Gives disk a volume label (use up to 11 characters).

The following table shows the standard sizes and formats for diskettes.

Standard diskette sizes and formats.

Size/Type	Amount of Data	Tracks	Sectors
5.25-inch, DS/DD	360K	40	9
3.5-inch, DS/DD	720K	80	9
5.25-inch, HD	1.2M	80	15

continues

167

Continued

Size/Type	Amount of Data	Tracks	Sectors
3.5-inch, HD	1.44M	80	18
3.5-inch, EHD	2.88M	80	36

No Switching! If you format a 360K 5.25-inch (DS/DD) disk in a 1.2M drive, remember to use that disk only in 1.2M drives from then on. These disks can't be read or written to by a 360K drive (reliably).

KEYS (OS/2 Only)

Recovers earlier commands during an OS/2 session. The closest DOS equivalent is DOSKEY.

KEYS=ON, where ON tells OS/2 to store commands for retrieval.

Other KEY commands are LIST, to show all commands from this session, or OFF—to tell OS/2 to stop storing commands. For example, to list commands entered in the current session (up to 64K), type KEYS=LIST.

MD or MKDIR (OS/2 and DOS)

Creates directories or subdirectories.

MD DATA, where DATA is the name of a new directory.

If you want to create a directory named MYDATA in the root directory of drive C while you're in another subdirectory, type

    MD C:\MYDATA

Getting Here from There You don't need to use the backslash (\) unless you want to create the directory in the root directory and you aren't already there. If you navigate using the drive object, long HPFS names are useful. If you navigate using the command line, you may decide that long names that contain spaces are more trouble than they're worth.

PATH (OS/2 and DOS)

Tells the system where to find an executable file (commands, programs, or batch files), if the system can't find the file internally or in the current directory. In OS/2, the PATH statement is usually included in CONFIG.SYS (while its DOS counterpart is usually set in AUTOEXEC.BAT).

> PATH C:\;C:\OS2;C:\OS2\APPS, where the PATH command is telling the system to look in the root directory, the OS/2 directory, and an OS/2 application's subdirectory each time an executable file is needed.

Follow the (Yellow Brick) PATH Your PATH statement must include the drive and path of each directory you want to include, separated by semicolons. PATH looks for the file in the order you have listed each subdirectory. A PATH statement is limited to 127 characters.

PROMPT (OS/2 and DOS)

Displays or controls the way the command line prompt appears.

`PROMPT Today is $D`, where `Today is $D` returns the text `Today is` followed by the current date.

To change your prompt permanently, add a SET PROMPT statement to your CONFIG.SYS file. You can add special strings to your command prompt by typing `$` followed by a character which designates that string. The following table shows the special strings available.

Adding PROMPT command special strings.

You Type	The System Returns
$_	Carriage return
$A	Ampersand (&)
$B	Vertical bar (¦)
$D	Current date
$E	The escape character (ASCII 27)
$G	Greater-than sign (>)
$H	Backspace
$I	Adds a Help prompt line at the top of the screen
$L	Less-than sign (<)
$N	The current drive letter
$P	The current drive and directory
$Q	An equal sign (=)
$R	A return code (error level)
$S	A space

You Type	The System Returns
$T	The current time
$V	The OS/2 version number

RENAME (OS/2 and DOS)

Gives a new name to files or extensions.

REN *.BAK *.OLD, where *.BAK represents current file names with .BAK extensions and *.OLD represents files with their renamed extensions.

REN C:\CONFIG.OLD CONFIG.BAK, where c:\ is the path; the directory need not be specified for the new name.

Some Moving Advice   Don't use RENAME (used in OS/2 and virtual DOS sessions) to move files. Instead, use COPY or MOVE. MOVE works in OS/2 and in OS/2 virtual DOS sessions (but not in a specific DOS version). RENAME is often used to move files in DOS because DOS does not include a MOVE command.

REPLACE (OS/2 and DOS)

Substitutes specified files on one drive with files of the same name on another drive. You can also copy a list of files to a target drive without overwriting any files with the same name.

171

REPLACE C:MYDOC.DOC A:/U, where A: is the target drive and C: is the source drive; switch ensures that only new source files are copied.

REPLACE C:\DATA C:\DESCRIBE\DATA/A adds any files from the \DATA subdirectory that don't already exist in the \DESCRIBE\DATA subdirectory.

Switches

/A Copies only files that aren't already on the target drive. (You cannot use /A together with /U or /S.)

/F Halts processing if the source contains extended attributes and the target doesn't support them.

/P Adds a prompt to confirm each file copied.

/R Overwrites read-only files.

/S Replaces files on subdirectories.

/U Replaces only source files that are newer than the target.

/W Waits for you to insert a disk into the source drive.

RD or RMDIR

Deletes an empty directory or subdirectory.

RD C:\WORD, where WORD is the directory to be removed.

RD C:\TEST\MYFILES, where MYFILES is the subdirectory to be removed from the directory C:\TEST.

Bottoms Up! RD won't work unless you empty the directory first. Also, you can't remove the root directory, the current directory, or any directories affected by JOIN or SUBST.

RESTORE (OS/2 and DOS)

Returns files written to disk by the BACKUP command.

RESTORE A: C:\DATA*.DAT /M /S, where A: is the source drive and the root directory on drive C is the target. The /M switch limits restoration to files that have changed since last backup. The /S switch tells RESTORE to put *.DAT on their original subdirectory.

The source is the drive containing the backup disk, and the target is any valid file specification (including drive, directory, and/or wild-card names).

Switches

/A:*mm-dd-yy* Restores files to the target that last changed on or after the date you set (for example, when you want to revert to an earlier data set).

/B:*mm-dd-yy* Restores files to the target that last changed on or before the date you set (for example, when you want to update files on the target).

/D Displays the contents of backup disk without restoring.

173

/E:hh:mm:ss   Restores files to the target that are earlier than those on the source. (/E specifies the time, while /B specifies the date.)

/F   Stops RESTORE if extended attributes are on the source but aren't supported on the target.

/L:hh:mm:ss   Restores files on the target that last changed at or after the time you set. (Compare with /A, which lets you specify the date.)

/M   Restores files to the target disk that have changed since the last backup.

/N   Restores files from the source that aren't already on the target in any version.

/P   Prompts you to replace read-only files or files that have changed since the last backup.

/S   Restores subdirectories

The Name Really Counts!   You can restore only to the exact subdirectory. For instance, C:\DATA\FILE.DAT backed up to drive A can be restored to \DATA on any disk, but can't be restored to a directory named \DOC or \OLDFILES.

START (OS/2 Only)

Starts OS/2 programs in a different session.

START "COPY MYGAMES" COPY A:\GAMES*.* B:\BACK, where A:\GAMES is the source and B:\BACK is the target;

shows COPY MYGAMES as the program name in the new session.

Here is a more formal syntax for the START command:

START ["*window title*" [/K¦/C¦/N] [/F¦/B] /PGM [/FS¦/WIN¦/PM] [/MAX¦/MIN]] *command* [*params*], where *window title* is the name OS/2 displays in the title bar and in the Window list, *command* is any program file (.EXE, .COM, or .CMD), and *params* are any parameters needed for the command or program being run. (Items within brackets are optional, and items separated by a vertical bar are mutually exclusive—that is, you may choose only one from each set.)

A Whole Lotta Characters! You can have up to 60 characters in the name you want to display in the window list.

Switches

/K Starts the program through CMD.EXE, and keeps the session after the program finishes.

/C Starts the program through CMD.EXE and ends the session after the command finishes.

/N Starts the program directly (doesn't use CMD.EXE) and ends the session after the program finishes (the program can't be an internal CMD.EXE command, such as DIR).

/F Starts the program as a foreground session.

/B Starts the program as a background session.

175

/PGM Tells OS/2 that the quoted name that follows is actually the file name for the program being run, not a title.

/FS Runs full screen (OS/2, unless /DOS also is specified).

/WIN Starts in window (OS/2, unless /DOS also is specified).

/PM Runs the Presentation Manager application in the foreground.

/MAX Starts application maximized.

/MIN Starts application minimized.

Here are several more examples:

START /C/WIN/DOS/F/MAX D:\SIG\SIG.EXE starts Signature in a windowed, foreground, maximized, DOS session. If you want your objects to start maximized, you can replace their .EXE files with a .CMD file like the preceding.

START /F/MAX/C MR2.EXE starts MailReader/2 as a foreground, maximized session.

TIME (OS/2 and DOS)

Displays or sets the system clock.

TIME 23:01, where the time is set to 11:01 p.m.—you must use 24-hour "military" time.

TREE (OS/2 and DOS)

Shows subdirectories for an entire disk.

TREE D: /F, where D: is the source and /F is a switch showing files as well as the directory structure.

Details! Details!   Remember that a colon must follow the drive letter.

TYPE

Displays a file on-screen. This command is designed for displaying text (ASCII) files that do not contain binary or other control characters.

TYPE D:\DATA\WEST.DOC, where D:\DATA is a subdirectory holding WEST.DOC, the file to be displayed.

TYPE CONFIG.SYS ¦MORE, where the MORE filter is used to show the file one screenful at a time.

UNDELETE (OS/2 and DOS)

Recovers deleted files from the DELETE directory.

UNDELETE MY.TXT, where the MY.TXT file is recovered.

UNDELETE /L, where a switch is used to list all files that are recoverable.

177

Switches

/L   Lists all files on the directory that are available for undeleting.

/S   Includes files in subdirectories off the current directory.

/A   Automatic; suppresses the confirmation prompt.

/F   Clears files from the delete directory so they can't be undeleted.

First Things First   To use UNDELETE, the following line (or one similar) must be placed in your OS/2 CONFIG.SYS and OS/2-DOS AUTOEXEC.BAT files: `SET DELDIR=C:\DELETE,512;D:\DELETE,512`. 512 indicates the amount of disk space, in kilobytes, to reserve for a delete queue.

As you delete files, they are moved to the \DELETE directory and hidden. When a deletion would cause the size of that directory to go above the indicated size (512K here), files are removed from the start of the queue until there is enough room for the newly deleted file. If there's not enough room, the whole queue is replaced by that single file until the next deletion.

VER (OS/2 and DOS)

Displays the version of OS/2 or DOS being used. To display a current version of the operating system, type **VER** and press **Enter**.

VMDISK (DOS Only)

Copies an image of a bootable diskette to a file.

> `VMDISK A: C:\DOS5\DOSIMAGE`, where `A:` (a floppy disk drive) is the source and `C:\DOS5\DOSIMAGE` (a fixed disk plus the directory and file name where you want the image file to reside) is the target.

XCOPY (DOS and OS/2)

Copies groups of files or subdirectories.

> `XCOPY A:\MYFILES C:\ALLFILES`, where a new subdirectory—ALLFILES—is created on drive C: and all of the files from A:\MYFILES are copied into it.

> `XCOPY A:\MYFILES C:\ALLFILES /V`, where `/V` (a switch) verifies that each of the files is copied accurately.

Switches

`/A` Copies only archive files; leaves the Archive attribute turned on.

`/D:mm-dd-yy` Copies files last changed on or after this date.

`/E` When used with /S, copies subdirectories even if they are empty.

`/F` Causes XCOPY to fail if extended attributes can't be copied to target drive.

179

/M   Copies files with the Archive bit turned on only; turns the archive bit off in the source files.

/P   Prompts before copying each file.

/S   Copies files on any subdirectories.

/V   Verifies accurate writing to disk.

Index

Symbols

* (asterisk) wild card character, 37
.D (file extension), 113-114
_ (underscore) character, 72

A

accessing
   disks, 147
   Windows Enhanced mode, 134, 145
activating main menu bars, 154
active window, 35
Activities List applet, master planner file, specifying, 114-115, 118
adding fonts, 52-53, 95-96
Adobe Type 1 fonts, adding, 95-96
Adobe Type Manager (ATM), installing fonts, 140-142
Alarms applet
   opening, 115
   setting
      alarms, 115-116
      master planner file, 113
aliases, 87
Alt-F4 (Close) key combination, 151
Alt-F9 (Minimize) key combination, 152

Alt-F10 (Maximize) key combination, 152
Alt-0 (expand list box) key combination, 23
applets, 112
   Activities List, 114-115, 118
   Alarms, 113-116
   Calendar, 112-115, 118
   Chart, 120
   Clipboard, 109-111, 124
   Daily Planner, 112-114, 117
   Database, 119
   Diary Planner, 113
   Icon Editor, 123
   integrating, 112-115
   Monthly Planner, 114-117
   Picture Viewer, 121
   Planner Archive, 118
   Pulse, 123
   Seek and Scan Files, 124
   specifying master planner file, 114-115
   Spreadsheet, 120
   Sticky Pad, 121-122
   system, 123-124
   Terminal, 122
   To Do List, 119
   Tune Editor, 119
applications
   backups, 145
   migrating, 54-55
   printing from, 92

Windows
　adding, 139
　Adobe Type Manager
　　(ATM), 140-142
　Clipboard, 140
　closing, 135
　displaying, 135-136
　opening, 133-134
　printing, 140
　running, 132, 136-137
Arrange (Desktop) option, 14
arrow keys, 22
ATM, *see* Adobe Type Manager
AUTOEXEC.BAT file, 128

B

Backspace key, 108
BACKUP command, 144, 160-161
backups
　applications, 145
　disks, 143-145
Boot Manager, 2
　deleting, 150
　installing, 146
booting, 2
borders, 5
buttons
　Help, 39
　Maximize, 5, 17
　Minimize, 5, 17
　mouse, 8

C

C prompt, *see* command line
Calendar applet, master planner
　　file, specifying, 112-115, 118
cancelling commands, 154
carriage returns, suppressing, 130
cascading windows, 12
CD/CHDIR (change directory)
　command, 162

Chart applet, 120
clicking mouse, 9-11
Clipboard, 109-111, 124
　DOS sessions, 128-130
　in WIN-OS/2, 140
Clock Settings notebook, 46
Close command, 151
closing
　command line session, 83
　DOS command line session, 127
　objects, 16, 24
　windows, 151
　Windows applications, 135
color, changing, 47-48
Color Palette, 47-48
command line, 81
　accessing, 82
　closing session, 83
　DOS sessions
　　Clipboard techniques,
　　　128-131
　　closing, 127
　　opening, 126
　editing, 86-87
　　command stack, 87
　　modes, 88
　help, 39, 88-89
　opening sessions, 82-84
　running programs, 85-86
command prompt, *see* command
　　line
Command Prompts (System
　　folder) subfolder, 31
Command Reference (Information
　　folder) subfolder, 31
command stack, 87
commands
　BACKUP, 144, 160-161
　cancelling, 154
　CD/CHDIR (change directory),
　　162
　Close, 151
　COPY, 72, 162-163

Index

DATE, 163-164
DETACH, 164
DIR (directory), 164-165
DOSKEY, 168
ERASE/DEL, 165-166
EXIT, 166
FDISK, 63
FORMAT, 166-168
HELP, 88-89
interface, 26
KEYS, 87, 168
MD/MKDIR, 168-169
Open, 83-84, 151
PATH, 169
PMSEEK, 124
PROMPT, 170-171
RD/RMDIR, 172-173
RENAME, 171
REPLACE, 171-172
RESTORE, 173-174
START, 174-176
TIME, 176
TREE, 177
TYPE, 177
UNDELETE, 77-79, 177-178
VER, 178
VMDISK, 179
XCOPY, 179
CONFIG.SYS file, 128
configuring DOS, 128
context-sensitive menus, 14
COPY command, 72, 162-163
copying
  files
    between folders, 73-74
    from HPFS to FAT, 71-72
    keyboard/mouse shortcut, 74
  folders
    between folders, 73-74
    from HPFS to FAT, 71
  objects, 57-58, 155
  text, 109-111
    from DOS, 129
    with mouse, 130
country settings, changing, 45

Create options
  Another, 57
  Shadow (Desktop), 13
creating
  folders, 157
  objects, 55-56, 157-158
  shadows, 58, 156
  subdirectories, 80
Ctrl-\ (deselect all icons) key
    combination, 155
cursor
  keys, 22
  speed setting, changing, 42
cutting text, 110-111

D

Daily Planner applet, 112, 117
  creating, 113-114
  specifying master planner file, 114-115
Database applet, 119
DATE command, 163-164
deactivating main menu bar, 154
default desktop, 30
  Drive A folder, 32
  Information folder, 31
  Master Help Index folder, 32
  Minimized Window Viewer (MWV) folder, 32
  Printer folder, 32
  Shredder folder, 33
  Start Here folder, 30
  System folder, 30-31
  Templates folder, 32
Delete key, 108
deleting
  Boot Manager, 150
  fonts, 53
  High Performance File System (HPFS) partitions, 150
  objects, 76-77, 156
  OS/2 files, 148-149
  text, 108

183

Desktop, 4-6
  Drive A folder, 32
  help, 35
  Information folder, 31
  Master Help Index folder, 32, 36-39
  Minimized Window Viewer (MWV) folder, 32
  pop-up menu, 12
  Printer folder, 32
  Shredder folder, 33
  Start Here folder, 30
  System folder, 30-31
  Templates folder, 32
DETACH command, 164
Details view, 29, 68-69
Device Driver Install, 58
device drivers, installing, 58
devices, 4
Diary Planner applet, 113
DIR (directory) command, 164-165
directories
  displaying
    Details view, 68-69
    Icon view, 67-68
    Tree view, 66
  moving objects across, 75
Disable Spooler option, 94
DISKCOPY, 143
diskettes, formatting, 69-70
disks
  accessing, 147
  backups, 143-145
  write-protecting, 143
displaying
  directories
    Details view, 68-69
    Icon view, 67-68
    Tree view, 66
  folders
    Details view, 68-69
    Icon view, 67-68
    Tree view, 66

pop-up menus, 14, 23-24
views, 26-29
Window list, 23
Windows applications, 135-136
DOS
  command-line session
    Clipboard, 128-131
    closing, 127
    opening, 126
  configuring, 128
  emulating, 125
  switching to OS/2, 2
DOSKEY
  command, 168
  program, 87
double-clicking mouse, 11, 44
drag-and-drop, printing with, 92
dragging
  mouse, 9-11
  objects, 152
Drive A folder, 32
drivers, printer, 91
  selecting, 101
  settings, changing, 103
drives, 65-66
  copying files, 71-74
  Details view, 68-69
  formatting diskettes, 69-70
  Icon view, 67
  icons, 66
  objects
    deleting, 76-77
    moving, 75
    renaming, 79
  opening, 66
  subdirectories, creating, 80
  Tree view, 66
  undeleting objects, 77-79
Drives (System folder) subfolder, 30
Drives folder, 65-66
Dual Boot, installing, 2, 146

Index

E

EA DATA.SF files, 63
Edit Scheme window, 49
editing
    command line, 86-87
        command stack, 87
        modes, 88
    files, 105-106
    icons, 123
    schemes, 49-51
Editor window, scroll bars, 19
editors, 104
    Enhanced File Editor, 111
    System Editor, 105-111
Enable Spooler option, 95
Enhanced File Editor, 111
enhanced filenames, 86
Enhanced (Windows) mode, 134
Enter key, 22
ERASE/DEL command, 165-166
errors, file allocation, 7
executing operating systems, multiple, 148
EXIT command, 166
expanding hidden lists in windows, 154
Extended Attributes (EA), 62-63, 72

F

F1 (Help) function key, 34-35
FAT, *see* File Allocation Table
FDISK command, 63
File Allocation Table (FAT), 60-61, 146
    Extended Attributes (EA), 62-63
    files
        copying from High Performance File System (HPFS), 71-72
        naming, 63-64

files
    allocation errors, 7
    AUTOEXEC.BAT, 128
    CONFIG.SYS, 128
    copying
        between folders, 73-74
        from High Performance File System (HPFS) to File Allocation Table (FAT), 71-72
        keyboard/mouse shortcut, 74
    deleting, 76-77
    EA DATA.SF, 63
    editing System Editor, 105-106
    extensions
        .D, 113-114
        .MET, 121
        .PCX, 92
        .SPL, 121
        .TIF, 92
    fragmentation, 61
    management, 65
    master planner, 113
    moving, 75
    naming, 63-64, 86
    OS/2, 148-149
    profile control, 59
    README, 126
    saving, 109
    searching for, 124
    undeleting, 77-79
Find (Desktop) option, 13, 19
finding icons, 19
floppy disks, copying files from hard disk, 71-72
folders, 4, 56
    copying
        between folders, 73-74
        from High Performance File System (HPFS) to File Allocation Table (FAT), 71
    creating, 157
    deleting, 76-77

185

displaying
  Details view, 68-69
  Icon view, 67-68
  Tree view, 66
Drive A, 32
Drives, 65-66
Information, 31
Master Help Index, 32, 36-39
Minimized Window Viewer
  (MWV), 32
moving, 75
objects, 56-57
Printer, 32
Shredder, 33
Start Here, 30
System, 30-31
Template, 55-56
Templates, 32
Windows applications, 139
Font Palette, 51-52
fonts
  adding, 52-53
  Adobe Type Manager,
    installing, 142
  applying to window, 52
  cartridges, changing, 96
  deleting, 53
  printer, adding, 95
  soft, adding, 96
FORMAT command, 166-168
formatting diskettes, 69-70
fragmentation, 61

G

Games (System folder) subfolder, 31
General Protection Fault (GPF), 137
General tab, 43
Glossary (Information folder) subfolder, 31
GPF (General Protection Fault), 137

H

hard disk
  copying files to floppy disk, 71-72
  partitions, 63
help
  at command line, 39
  command line, 88-89
  Desktop, 35
  displaying, 38
  F1 function key, 34-35
  menu options, 35
  push buttons, 35
Help (Desktop) option, 13
Help button, 39
HELP command, 88-89
hidden lists, expanding, 154
High Performance File System
  (HPFS), 60-61
  Extended Attributes (EA), 62-63
  files, 63-64
    copying to File Allocation
      Table (FAT), 71-72
    naming, 63-64
  installing, 144
  partitions, deleting, 150
hot links, 38
HPFS, *see* High Performance File
  System
hypertext, 38

I

Icon Editor applet, 123
Icon view, displaying, 27, 67-68
icons, 4
  editing, 123
  finding, 19
  names, changing, 43
  object, 4
  Title Bar, 4

Index

Information folder, 31
Insert mode, 107
inserting text, 107
insertion point, moving, 106-107
installing
    ATM fonts, 142
    Boot Manager, 146
    device drivers, 58
    Dual Boot, 146
    High Performance File System (HPFS), 144
    OS/2 components, 58, 145
integrating applets, 112-115
interfaces, printer, 26, 91
InterFAXability printer driver, 91

K

key combinations, 22
    Alt-F4 (Close), 151
    Alt-F9 (Minimize), 152
    Alt-F10 (Maximize), 152
    Alt-0 (expand list box), 23
    Ctrl-\ (deselect icons), 155
    Shift-Tab, 22
Keyboard Settings notebook, 42
keyboards
    changing, 40-41
        consecutive key assignments, setting, 43
        cursor settings, speed, 42
        remapping keys, 43
    insertion point, moving, 106
    menus, displaying, 23-24
    objects
        closing, 24
        naming, 43
        opening, 24
    selecting text, 108
    Window list, displaying, 23
    windows
        moving, 25
        resizing, 24-25
        restoring, 25

keys
    arrow, 22
    Backspace, 108
    consecutive key assignments, setting, 43
    Delete, 108
    Enter, 22
    F1 (Help), 34-35
    remapping, 43
    Tab, 21
KEYS command, 87, 168
KEYS OFF editing mode, 88
KEYS ON editing mode, 88

L-M

Lockup now (Desktop) option, 13

main menu bars, 154
Mappings tab, 43-45
Master Help Index folder, 32, 36-39
master planner file, 113-115
Maximize button, 5, 17
maximizing windows, 25
MD/MKDIR command, 168-169
menus
    context-sensitive, 14
    options, help, 35
    pop-up, 12-14
        Desktop, 12
        displaying, 14, 23-24
.MET file extension, 121
migrating applications, 54-55
Minimize button, 5, 17
Minimized Window Viewer (MWV) folder, 32
minimizing windows, 24
modes
    Enhanced (Windows), 134
    Insert, 107
    KEYS OFF, 88
    KEYS ON, 88
    Overtype, 107

187

Monthly Planner applet, master
    planner file, specifying,
    114-117
mouse
    buttons, 8, 44
    clicking, 9-11
    double-clicking, 11
    dragging, 9-11
    pointing, 9
    speed, setting, 44
    text
        copying, 130
        pasting, 131
        selecting, 107-108
mouse pointer, 4, 9
Mouse Settings notebook, 44
moving
    insertion point, 106-107
    objects, 18-19, 75
    objects among folders, 56-57
    windows, 25
    within screens, 21-23

N

naming
    files, 63-64, 86
    icons, 43
    objects, 43
notebooks, 40
    Clock Settings, 46
    Keyboard Settings, 42
    Mouse Settings, 44

O

objects, 8
    closing, 16, 24
    color, changing, 47-48
    copying, 57-58, 155
    creating, 55-56
    deleting, 76-77, 156
    dragging, 152

help, 35
icons, 4
moving, 18-19, 75
moving among folders, 56-57
names, changing, 43
open, 4
opening, 15-16, 24
pop-up menus, 12-14
printers, 99, 158
    controlling display, 102
    putting print job on hold, 99
    renaming, 102
    viewing print jobs, 99
programs, 157
renaming, 79, 158
selected, 4
shadows, 156
Open (Desktop) option, 13
Open command, 83-84, 151
open object, 4
opening
    Alarms applet, 115
    command line sessions,
        multiple, 82-84
    DOS command line sessions,
        126
    drives, 66
    Master Help Index folder, 36
    objects, 15-16, 24
    System Editor, 105
    windows, 151
    Windows applications, 133-134
operating systems, 2, 148
options, Desktop pop-up menu, 13
OS/2 files
    deleting, 148-149
    installing, 145
    opening screen, 3-5
    shutting down, 6-7
    starting, 1-3
    switching to DOS, 2
    uninstalling, 148-150
Overtype mode, 107

Index

P

palettes
   Color, 47-48
   Font, 51-52
   Scheme, 49-51
partitions, 63
pasting text, 110-111
   from DOS, 130
   with mouse, 131
PATH command, 169
.PCX file extension, 92
Picture Viewer applet, 121
Planner Archive applet, 118
PMSEEK command, 124
PMSHELL.EXE, *see* Workplace Shell (WPS)
pointing mouse, 9
pop-up menus, 12-14
   Desktop, 12
   displaying, 14, 23-24
ports, printer, selecting, 102
Presentation Manager (PM), 34
Printer folder, 32
printers
   changing characteristics, 101-103
   drivers, 91
      selecting, 101
      settings, changing, 103
   fonts, adding, 95
   interfaces, 91
   objects
      controlling display, 102
      creating, 158
      pausing print jobs, 99
      renaming, 102
      viewing print jobs, 99
   ports, selecting, 102
   queues, options, 98, 102
printing, 98
   cancelling print job, 100
   drag-and-drop method, 92
   from applications, 92
   in WIN-OS/2, 140
   pausing, 99
   reordering, 99-100
   viewing print job, 99
Productivity (System folder) subfolder, 31
profile control files, 59
profiles, 122
program objects, creating, 157
programs
   DOSKEY, 87
   running, 85-86
PROMPT command, 170-171
Pulse applet, 123
push buttons, help, 35

R

RD/RMDIR command, 172-173
README file, 126
Refresh (Desktop) option, 13
RENAME command, 171
renaming objects, 79, 102, 158
REPLACE command, 171-172
resizing windows, 17-18, 25, 152
RESTORE command, 173-174
restoring windows, 17, 25
REXX Information (Information folder) subfolder, 31
rotating open tasks, 153
running programs, Windows applications, 85-86, 132-133, 136-137

S

saving files, 109
Scheme Palette, 49-51
schemes, editing, 49-51

189

screens
    moving within, 21-23
    opening, 3-5
scroll bars, 19
searching
    for files, 124
    windows, 154
Seek and Scan Files applet, 124
Select (Desktop) option, 14
selecting
    objects, 4
    text, 107-108
selection letters, 22
Selective Install, 58
Setup tab, 44-45
shadows, 13, 57-58, 156
Shift-Tab key combination, 22
Shredder folder, 33
Shut down (Desktop) option, 13
shutting down OS/2, 6-7
soft fonts, adding, 96
Sort (Desktop) option, 14
sound, controlling, 45
space bar, 22
Special Needs tab, 43
specifying master planner file, 114-115
.SPL file extension, 121
Spooler, 93
    disabling, 94
    enabling, 95
    file location, setting, 94
Spreadsheet applet, 120
START command, 174-176
Start Here folder, 30
starting OS/2, 1-3
Startup (System folder) subfolder, 30
Sticky Pad applet, 121-122
subdirectories, 80
subfolders
    Command Prompts, 31
    Command Reference, 31
    Drives, 30

Games, 31
Glossary, 31
Productivity, 31
REXX Information, 31
Startup, 30
System Startup, 31
Tutorial, 31
symbols, 120
SYS error message box, 39
system applets, 123-124
System Clock, 46
System Editor
    files
        editing, 105-106
        saving, 109
    insertion point, moving, 106-107
    opening, 105
    text
        copying, 109-111
        cutting, 110-111
        deleting, 108
        inserting, 107
        pasting, 110-111
        selecting, 107-108
System folder, 30-31
System Setup (System folder) subfolder, 31

T

Tab key, 21
tabs, 40
    General, 43
    Mappings, 43-45
    Setup, 44-45
    Special Needs, 43
    Timing, 42
    Timings, 44
tasks, 4, 11-12
templates, 49, 55-56
Templates folder, 32, 55-56
Terminal applet, 122

text
  copying, 109-111
    from DOS, 129
    with mouse, 130
  cutting, 110-111
  deleting, 108
  inserting, 107
  pasting, 110-111
    from DOS, 130
    with mouse, 131
  selecting, 107-108
.TIF file extension, 92
tiling windows, 12
TIME command, 176
Timings tab, 42-44
title bar, 5
Title Bar icon, 4
To Do List applet, 119
TREE command, 177
Tree view, displaying, 28, 66
Tune Editor applet, 119
Tutorial (Information folder)
    subfolder, 31
TYPE command, 177

U

UAE (Unrecoverable Application
    Error), 137
UNDELETE command, 77-79,
    177-178
undeleting files, 77-79
underscore (_) character, 72
uninstalling OS/2, 148-150
Unrecoverable Application Error
    (UAE), 137

V

VDM (virtual DOS machines),
    125-126
VER command, 178

viewing
  print jobs, 99
  README file, 126
views, 26
  Details, 29, 68-69
  Icon, 27, 67-68
  Tree, 28, 66
virtual DOS machines, *see* VDM
VMDISK command, 179
volume labels, 70

W

wild card characters, 37
WIN-OS/2 Windows application,
    139
  adding, 139
  Clipboard, 140
  closing, 135
  configuring, 138
  opening, 133-134
  printing, 140
  running, 132-133
Windows
  applications
    adding, 139
    Adobe Type Manager
      (ATM), 140-142
    Clipboard, 140
    closing, 135
    displaying, 135-136
    opening, 133-134
    printing, 140
    running, 132-133, 136-137
  configuring, 138
  Enhanced mode, 134, 145
  General Protection Fault (GPF),
    137
  list, 11-12, 23
  printing applications, 140
  Unrecoverable Application
    Error (UAE), 137

windows, 4-5
  active, 35
  arranging, 11-12
  cascading, 12
  closing, 151
  Edit Scheme, 49
  Editor scroll bars, 19
  fonts, applying, 52
  hidden lists, expanding, 154
  maximizing, 17, 25
  minimizing, 17, 24
  moving, 25
  opening, 151
  resizing, 17-18, 25, 152
  restoring, 17, 25
  searching, 154
  tiling, 12
  titles, 5
WinFax printer driver, 91
Work Area, 56
Workplace Shell (WPS) views, 15-16
  Details, 29
  Icon, 27
  Tree, 28
WPS, *see* Workplace Shell
write-protecting disks, 143

X

XCOPY command, 179